A CALL TO
PRAYER
FOR A
NATION
AT WAR

PRAYERS OF BLESSING
AND PROTECTION
FOR THOSE WHO SERVE

WHITE STONE BOOKS
LAKELAND, FLORIDA

DEDICATED to the men, women, and families of the United States Armed Forces—the strong few who find the courage to stand against the evils of tyranny and terrorism and who are ready even to sacrifice their lives to defend our nation.

AND

To those who relentlessly pray for the protection, encouragement, and guidance of our Armed Forces and nation; these prayer warriors who fight in the battlefield of the spiritual realm.

A CALL TO
PRAYER
FOR A
NATION
AT WAR

PRAYERS OF BLESSING
AND PROTECTION
FOR THOSE WHO SERVE

07 06 05 04 03   10 9 8 7 6 5 4 3 2

A Call to Prayer for a Nation at War
ISBN 1-59379-009-0
Copyright © 2003 by White Stone Books, Inc.
Published by White Stone Books, Inc.
P.O. Box 2835
Lakeland, Florida

CONTENTS

PERSONAL PRAYERS

I WANT TO THANK each and every member of our Armed Forces for your courage to stand against the evils that threaten the safety of our nation and the world, for your willingness to stand for what you believe, and for your sacrifices made to ensure the freedom of our children.

Thank you for your endless dedication to fulfill the mission God has called you to. Your courage is an inspiration to us and we are honored to stand beside you in prayer and in patriotic spirit. We pray that God will encourage, strengthen, and protect you and your family.

Sincerely,
The Publisher
WHITE STONE BOOKS

INTRODUCTION

A CALL TO PRAYER

FAITH, courage, and prayer birthed our great nation and successfully guided America through more than two hundred years of war, natural disaster, and national crisis.

Prayer is a freedom guaranteed to us by our Constitution, and a God-given right to all humanity. The opportunity to pray is a privilege, honor, and sacred duty.

And never has this privilege and duty been more necessary than now.

The forces of evil are waging war against our freedom. Terrorism has shed blood on American soil. Tyrants and terrorists from other lands are ever dedicated to undermine the safety and stability of our nation.

Prayer for our nation is our most powerful defense.

Now is the time to unite as a nation, standing with our troops in battle through prayer.

Will *you* answer this call to prayer? For your President? His cabinet and advisors? For Congress? For military leaders? Most of all, will you answer this call for your soldiers on the frontlines of battle?

We often fail to answer the call to prayer, because we are unsure how to pray and don't know where to turn for guidance. This book is designed to provide a variety of helps that will empower your prayer life.

- Three sections of specific scriptural prayers that are particularly relevant in this time of war; prayers for the military, prayers for the nation, and prayers for your own life.

- Inspiring prayers, thoughts, quotes, stories, and speeches from history—and today.

- A 31-day devotional guide on prayer to help attune your mind and spirit to God's provision in this time of need.

The prayers that form the heart of this book are each carefully based on Bible passages so that you can pray with confidence, knowing you are praying God's will for this nation.

So, will you answer the call to prayer now? Make a commitment to pray daily for your nation. Pray the prayers found in these pages with heart, purpose, and passion. Your heavenly Father is listening. He loves you and this nation.

THE STATE OF THE UNION ADDRESS
BY
PRESIDENT GEORGE W. BUSH
JANUARY 2003

YOU AND I serve our country in a time of great consequence. We will work for a prosperity that is broadly shared, and we will answer every danger and every enemy that threatens the American people.

The qualities of courage and compassion that we strive for in America also determine our conduct abroad. The American flag stands for more than our power and our interests. Our founders dedicated this country to the cause of human dignity, the rights of every person and the possibilities of every life. This conviction leads us into the world to help the afflicted, and defend the peace, and confound the designs of evil men.

As our nation moves troops and builds alliances to make our world safer, we must also remember our calling, as a blessed country, is to make the world better.

There are days when our fellow citizens do not hear news about the war on terror. There's never a day when I do not learn of another threat, or receive reports of operations in progress or give an order in this global war against a scattered network of killers.

The war goes on, and we are winning. One by one the terrorists are learning the meaning of American justice. As we fight this war, we will remember where it began: here, in our own country. This government is taking unprecedented measures to protect our people and defend our homeland.

Our war against terror is a contest of will in which perseverance is power. In the ruins of two towers, at the western wall of the Pentagon, on a field in Pennsylvania, this nation made a pledge, and we renew that pledge tonight: Whatever the duration of this struggle and whatever the difficulties, we will not permit the triumph of violence in the affairs of men; free people will set the course of history.

Today, the gravest danger in the war on terror, the gravest danger facing America and the world, is outlaw regimes that seek and possess nuclear, chemical and biological weapons. These regimes could use such weapons for blackmail, terror and mass murder. They could also give or sell those weapons to terrorist allies, who would use them without the least hesitation.

Throughout the 20th century, small groups of men seized control of great nations, built armies and arsenals, and set out to dominate the weak and intimidate the world. In each case, their ambitions of cruelty and murder had no limit. In each case, the ambitions of Hitlerism, militarism and communism were defeated by the will of free peoples, by the strength of great alliances and by the might of the United States of America.

Now, in this century, the ideology of power and domination has appeared again and seeks to gain the ultimate weapons of terror. Once again, this nation and our friends are all that stand between a world at peace, and a world of chaos and constant alarm. Once again, we are called to defend the safety of our people and the hopes of all mankind. And we accept this responsibility.

I have a message for the men and women who will keep the peace, members of the American armed forces. Many of you are assembling in or near the Middle East, and some crucial hours may lay ahead. In those hours, the success of our cause will depend on you. Your training has prepared you. Your honor will guide you. You believe in America and America believes in you.

Sending Americans into battle is the most profound decision a president can make. The technologies of war have changed. The risks and suffering of war have not. For the brave Americans who bear the risk, no victory is free from sorrow. This nation fights reluctantly, because we know the cost, and we dread the days of mourning that always come.

We seek peace. We strive for peace. And sometimes peace must be defended. A future lived at the mercy of terrible threats is no peace at all. If war is forced upon us, we will fight in a just cause and by just means, sparing, in every way we can, the innocent. And if war is forced upon us, we will fight with the full force and might of the United States military, and we will prevail.

Americans are a resolute people, who have risen to every test of our time. Adversity has revealed the character of our country, to the world, and to ourselves. America is a strong nation and honorable in the use of our strength. We exercise power without conquest, and we sacrifice for the liberty of strangers.

AMERICANS ARE A FREE PEOPLE, who know that freedom is the right of every person and the future of every nation. The liberty we prize is not America's gift to the world; it is God's gift to humanity.

WE AMERICANS HAVE FAITH in ourselves, but not in ourselves alone. We do not claim to know all the ways of Providence, yet we can trust in them, placing our confidence in the loving God behind all of life and all of history.

MAY HE GUIDE US NOW, and may God continue to bless the United States of America.

THANK YOU.

The earnest prayer
of a righteous person
has great power
and wonderful results.

JAMES 5:16

*More things are
wrought by prayer
than this world dreams of.*

—ALFRED, LORD TENNYSON

PRAYERS
FOR THE
MILITARY

*And let us not trust to human effort
alone, but humbly acknowledging the
power and goodness of Almighty God,
who presides over the destiny of nations,
and who has at times been revealed
in our country's history; let us invoke
His aid and His blessings upon our labors.*

—GROVER CLEVELAND

1

DELIVER ME FROM MY ENEMIES,
O God; protect me from those
who rise up against me.

PSALM 59:1

BUT IN THAT COMING DAY,
no weapon turned against you will succeed.
And everyone who tells lies in court will be
brought to justice. These benefits are enjoyed
by the servants of the Lord; their vindication
will come from me. I, the Lord, have spoken!

ISAIAH 54:17

*Let us unite in imploring the
Supreme Ruler of Nations to spread
His holy protection over these United States.*

—GEORGE WASHINGTON

A PRAYER FOR PROTECTION

DEAR HEAVENLY FATHER, I pray for protection for the men and women of our military. I know that You said in Your Word that You would never leave us nor forsake us. I believe that Your angels go before our soldiers to protect them and keep them from harm and danger of any kind.

Lord, Your Word says that You hide us under Your wings, that no evil shall befall us, and that no plague nor calamity shall come near us.

I pray for safety over each military operation. Wherever our troops go and whatever they do, I thank You that they operate in Your divine protection. I pray for safety as they travel by air, sea, and land to every destination. I pray that You would protect them from the enemy, friendly fire, or accidents of any kind. I pray that You would protect them from any threats of physical, mental, or emotional violence.

Father, I pray for Your peace that passes all understanding. May it guard the hearts and minds of our soldiers. Thank You for Your protection in every area of their lives.

Amen.

A HOUSE IS BUILT BY WISDOM
and becomes strong through good sense.

PROVERBS 24:3

IF YOU NEED WISDOM—if you want to
know what God wants you to do—ask him, and he
will gladly tell you. He will not resent your asking.
But when you ask him, be sure that you really expect
him to answer, for a doubtful mind is as unsettled as
a wave of the sea that is driven and tossed by the wind.

JAMES 1:5,6

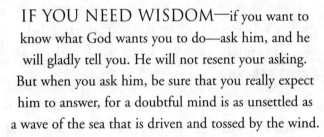

*God, give us grace to accept with serenity
the things that cannot be changed,
courage to change the things
which should be changed,
and the wisdom to distinguish
the one from the other.*

—THE SERENITY PRAYER

A PRAYER FOR WISDOM FOR OUR MILITARY LEADERS

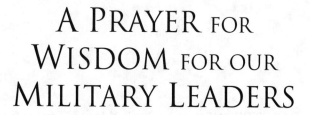

DEAR LORD JESUS, please bless those who are in leadership positions in our military. Lord, Your Word says that we can ask for wisdom and that You will freely give it, and I ask You to give them incredible wisdom!

Help them to comprehend and interpret all intelligence reports they receive. Lord, give them guidance concerning every decision they are called upon to make. Give them the wisdom and understanding beyond their own natural ability. Surround them with wise and prudent council. Give them the ability to discern and perceive in their spirit what they might not understand through their intellect.

If they don't know You, let them find a personal relationship with Christ so they can be righteous in Your sight. Please protect them and bless their families.

Amen.

BE STRONG AND COURAGEOUS.

Do not be afraid or terrified because of them,
for the LORD your God goes with you;
he will never leave you nor forsake you.

DEUTERONOMY 31:6

HAVE I NOT COMMANDED YOU?

Be strong and courageous. Do not be terrified;
do not be discouraged, for the LORD your God
will be with you wherever you go.

JOSHUA 1:9

*One man with courage
makes a majority.*

—ANDREW JACKSON

A Prayer for Courage

FATHER, in Jesus' name I lift up the men and women of our Armed Forces who are heading into battle. I ask You to help them face our adversaries boldly and confidently.

In Deuteronomy, Your Word says, "Be strong and courageous. Do not be afraid or terrified of them, for the LORD your God goes with you; I will never leave you nor forsake you." Father, give them confidence to go forth boldly without fear. Give them grace and mercy in their time of trouble.

Cause courage to rise up bold and wax strong in the hearts of our military. Help all of our military personnel not to be discouraged, fearful, or intimidated. Let all fears, worries, and doubts be replaced with courage, strength, and boldness.

I boldly proclaim that our military is confident because of Your promises. Thank You that our troops can operate in courage in every area of their lives, not because of who they are, but because of who You are in them. Let Your Word bring confidence and completion in each life.

Amen.

THOSE WHO LIVE in the shelter of the Most High will find rest in the shadow of the Almighty. This I declare of the Lord: He alone is my refuge, my place of safety; he is my God, and I am trusting him. For he will rescue you from every trap and protect you from the fatal plague. He will shield you with his wings. He will shelter you with his feathers. His faithful promises are your armor and protection. Do not be afraid of the terrors of the night, nor fear the dangers of the day, nor dread the plague that stalks in darkness, nor the disaster that strikes at midday. Though a thousand fall at your side, though ten thousand are dying around you, these evils will not touch you. But you will see it with your eyes; you will see how the wicked are punished.

PSALM 91:1-8

FINALLY, I brought you into the land of the Amorites on the east side of the Jordan. They fought against you, but I gave you victory over them, and you took possession of their land.

JOSHUA 24:8 (NLT)

The eyes of the world are upon you. The hopes and prayers of liberty-loving people everywhere march with you. I have full confidence in your courage, devotion to duty, and skill in battle. We will accept nothing less than full victory!

—DWIGHT D. EISENHOWER

A PRAYER FOR SUCCESSFUL MISSIONS

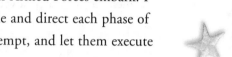

L ORD, I pray for the success of the missions on which the members of our Armed Forces embark. I pray that You would guide and direct each phase of every operation our soldiers attempt, and let them execute each with excellence.

Keep them safe, Lord, whether they are flying combat missions over hostile forces, fighting on the ground, or simply transporting food or supplies from one point to another—let all of their missions be successful and productive.

Let the planning of each operation be thoughtful and complete; give those in charge of the planning, wisdom, and the information they need to make good decisions.

I pray that You would especially be with those individuals who are on dangerous missions that put them in harm's way. Bless them and protect them; let Your angels surround them. Bring them all home safely.

Amen.

BY FAITH THESE PEOPLE overthrew kingdoms, ruled with justice, and received what God had promised them. They shut the mouths of lions, quenched the flames of fire, and escaped death by the edge of the sword. Their weakness was turned to strength. They became strong in battle and put whole armies to flight. Women received their loved ones back again from death.

HEBREWS 11:33-35 (NLT)

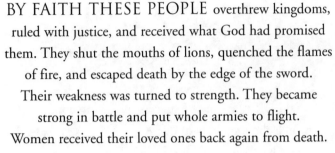

GOD OUR FATHER LOVES US. He is kind and has given us eternal comfort and a wonderful hope. We pray that our Lord Jesus Christ and God our Father will encourage you and help you always to do and say the right thing.

2 THESSALONIANS 2:16,17 (CEV)

Never give in, never give in, never, never, never, never—in nothing, great or small, large or petty—never give in except to convictions of honor and good sense.

—SIR WINSTON CHURCHILL

A Prayer for Encouragement

LORD, I pray that You would help the men and women of our military overcome discouraging situations. Help them remember that there is no problem too big, no hurt too deep, and no mistake too bad that You cannot provide the power, strength, and wisdom to overcome it.

In Your Word it says You will never leave us or forsake us. In the Psalms, David praises You for turning his mourning into dancing. Help the individuals in our Armed Forces to remember these promises and to praise You even in difficult situations!

Encourage these people who put their lives between the enemy and our nation. Let them know that their contribution is worthwhile, appreciated, and noticed. Encourage them to be emissaries for You and to represent You with an attitude of pride. Be the joy of their lives, Lord, and keep their eyes on You instead of circumstances that might get them down.

Amen.

CAN ANYTHING EVER separate us from Christ's love? Does it mean he no longer loves us if we have trouble or calamity, or are persecuted, or are hungry or cold or in danger or threatened with death? (Even the Scriptures say, 'For your sake we are killed every day; we are being slaughtered like sheep.') No, despite all these things, overwhelming victory is ours through Christ, who loved us. And I am convinced that nothing can ever separate us from his love. Death can't, and life can't. The angels can't, and the demons can't. Our fears for today, our worries about tomorrow, and even the powers of hell can't keep God's love away. Whether we are high above the sky or in the deepest ocean, nothing in all creation will ever be able to separate us from the love of God that is revealed in Christ Jesus our Lord.

ROMANS 8:35-39 (NLT)

FOR YOU KNOW that God paid a ransom to save you from the empty life you inherited from your ancestors. And the ransom he paid was not mere gold or silver. He paid for you with the precious lifeblood of Christ, the sinless, spotless Lamb of God. God chose him for this purpose long before the world began, but now in these final days, he was sent to the earth for all to see. And he did this for you.

1 PETER 1:17 (NLT)

There are no atheists in foxholes.
—FATHER WILLIAM THOMAS CUMMINGS

A Prayer
for Salvation
in our Military

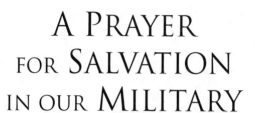

LORD, I pray for those men and women in our Armed Forces who don't know You as their personal Lord and Savior. I pray that Your Holy Spirit will draw them to You so they can inherit eternal life!

Your Word says that You came to save the world, Jesus, not to condemn it, and I pray that Your saving grace would find thousands of individuals in our military right this minute who don't know You. Save their souls, Lord, and put them on a right track with You.

Lord, many of these unsaved men and women might think of You as a mean and vengeful God, or perhaps as a cruelly indifferent creator. Show them Your love, Lord, and put people in their paths who will show them Your love in action. Convict them of their sins and turn them from their ways; help them to love You!

Lord, I ask that You save those individuals who have used Your name in vain or as a curse—let them instead utter the name of Jesus as praise and as a prayer to You when they are in crisis. Have mercy on them!

Amen.

'THEY WILL FIGHT AGAINST YOU,
but they shall not prevail against you.
For I am with you,' says the Lord, 'to deliver you.'
JEREMIAH 1:19 (NLT)

YE ARE OF GOD, little children,
and have overcome them: because greater is
he that is in you, than he that is in the world.
1 JOHN 4:4 (NLT)

*Faith is a living and unshakable
confidence, a belief in the grace of
God so assured that a man would
die a thousand deaths for its sake.*
—MARTIN LUTHER

A PRAYER FOR CHRISTIANS IN THE ARMED FORCES

LORD, I know that there are many people in our military who know You as Lord. I acknowledge that it might not be easy for them to be good witnesses for You, in other nations where you are defied—alongside fellow soldiers, some who do not know You. Give these soldiers for Christ a good testimony! Lord, let them stand out as different from those around them—and let that difference draw men and women to You for salvation!

Lord, the military takes Your people all over the globe, and I pray that they would use their opportunities to be shining lamps for You in foreign lands. Let them be salt and light to a dying world and let their very presence in a country be a powerful evangelistic tool. Give them hearts for sharing You, even if it is simply through their daily actions.

Protect Your saints in the Armed Forces, Lord, and let them be bold in confessing You before men so You can openly reward them. Promote them and provide for them, Lord, and bless their families at home. Let those of us here never cease to pray for them.

Amen.

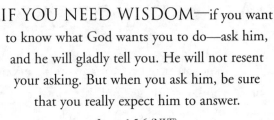

IF YOU NEED WISDOM—if you want
to know what God wants you to do—ask him,
and he will gladly tell you. He will not resent
your asking. But when you ask him, be sure
that you really expect him to answer.

JAMES 1:5,6 (NLT)

TRUST IN THE LORD with all your heart;
do not depend on your own understanding.
Seek his will in all you do, and he will direct your paths.

PROVERBS 3:5

Do not pray for easy lives,
pray for stronger men. Do not pray
for tasks equal to your powers,
but for powers equal to your tasks.

—PHILLIPS BROOKS

A PRAYER FOR DECISIONS MADE UNDER STRESS AND IN CRISIS

LORD, Your Word says that You are not the author of confusion, and I ask that You would superintend the decisions those in our military make during periods of stress and in crisis. Let them have sound minds to maintain peace under pressure.

Lord, let not the individuals in our military become fearful, anxious, or overwhelmed in situations of crisis. Help our soldiers to not react in confusion, worry, or desperation.

Lord Jesus, thank You for giving them Your peace, and let Your peace, which surpasses all understanding, guard their hearts and minds. Enable them to face every situation they encounter with confidence in You and Your power to deliver them.

Keep their hearts from being troubled, and do not let them give in to a spirit of fear but to embrace the spirit of power, love, and a sound mind that You have given them.

Give our military leaders clear minds and hearts able to listen to You. Let their confidence and trust reside in You, their God. Even in the heat of battle, help their every action to be guided by You. Let them confidently and boldly proclaim Your promises when they are in stressful or dangerous situations.

Amen.

A KINGDOM AT WAR
with itself will collapse.
A home divided against itself is doomed.

MARK 3:23 (NLT)

AS IRON SHARPENS IRON,
so a man sharpens the countenance of his friend.

PROVERBS 27:17 (NKJV)

*The service we render others is the rent
we pay for our room on earth.*

—WILFRED GRENFELL

A Prayer for Cooperation

Lord, help the various branches of our military to be able to work together and communicate effectively. Help them to share similar goals and to agree on reasonable means for accomplishing their objectives. Especially bless those involved in Homeland Defense, helping them accurately share vital information on threats and opportunities.

Lord, help the various departments in our military organizations to function efficiently. Please let miscommunication never cost lives or give our enemies an advantage. Let the branches of our military keep open lines of communication and facilitate one another's objectives.

I pray that the literal means of communication—the equipment and operators who run and maintain it—would work flawlessly, and let our troops have what they need in order to cooperate with one another.

Amen.

BUT FOR YOU WHO FEAR MY NAME,
the Sun of Righteousness will rise with healing
in his wings. And you will go free,
leaping with joy like calves let out to pasture.

MALACHI 4:2

I AM THE LORD YOUR GOD,
and I cure your diseases. If you obey me by doing
right and by following my laws and teachings, I won't
punish you with the diseases I sent on the Egyptians.

EXODUS 15:26

I treated him, God cured him.

—AMBROISE PARÉ

A Prayer for Healing

L ORD, the Bible tells us that You are the author of our
healing, and I believe that includes both physical and
less tangible forms of healing. Lord, first I address those
people who have suffered physical injuries in our Armed
Forces; I pray that they would recover quickly from their
wounds and suffer no lasting impairment. Let their medica-
tions function perfectly and without side effects.

Lord, I also ask that You would heal those who are hurt in
mind or spirit. Lord, bless those individuals who suffer from
such conditions as post traumatic stress syndrome, and give
them peace that surpasses understanding. Lord, comfort those
who have been hurt emotionally, those who have been scared
by battle or other trauma. Let them find abundant grace for
their daily lives and to recover quickly from the effects of the
adverse circumstances that hurt them.

You are the God of the living and not the dead, and I pray
that abundant life would be the order of the day for the men
and women of our Armed Forces.

Amen.

A BODY ISN'T REALLY A BODY,

unless there is more than one part. It takes many parts
to make a single body. That's why the eyes cannot say
they don't need the hands. That's also why the head cannot
say it doesn't need the feet. In fact, we cannot get along
without the parts of the body that seem to be the weakest.

1 CORINTHIANS 12:19-22 (CEV)

WORK HARD, but not just to please your masters

when they are watching. As slaves of Christ, do the will
of God with all your heart. Work with enthusiasm,
as though you were working for the Lord rather than for
people. Remember that the Lord will reward each one of us
for the good we do, whether we are slaves or free.

EPHESIANS 6:6-8 (NLT)

*We are ready to sacrifice ourselves for
our country and our God. We do not ask,
individually, for our safe return.
But we earnestly pray that You will help
each of us to do his full duty. Permit none
of us to fail a comrade in the fight.*

—DWIGHT D. EISENHOWER

A Prayer for Excellence

F ATHER GOD, I pray for a pursuit of excellence to be typical of our military. I ask that the people involved in every department and branch of our military would strive to be the best they can be and to perform their duties skillfully.

Lord, help them to see that each contribution is important—especially those individuals who might feel as though their duties aren't glamorous or vital. Bless those who are involved with logistics; help them plan and deliver the necessary materials to provide everything our soldiers need.

Lord, help them to work as unto You, and let them enjoy their jobs and find fulfillment in them. Bless everything they set their hands to and help them give You the glory for the evident favor among men You give them.

Amen.

GOD IS OUR REFUGE and strength, always ready to help in times of trouble. So we will not fear, even if earthquakes come and the mountains crumble into the sea.

PSALM 46:1 (NLT)

THE LORD IS YOUR PROTECTOR, and he won't go to sleep or let you stumble. The protector of Israel doesn't doze or ever get drowsy. The Lord is your protector, there at your right side to shade you from the sun. You won't be harmed by the sun during the day or by the moon at night. The Lord will protect you and keep you safe from all dangers. The Lord will protect you now and always wherever you go.

PSALM 121:3-8 (CEV)

Whatever the duration of this struggle and whatever the difficulties, we will not permit the triumph of violence in the affairs of men; free people will set the course of history.

—GEORGE W. BUSH

A PRAYER FOR SAFETY

L ORD, I come before You on behalf of the men and
women of our Armed Forces to ask You to preserve
them and keep them safe. Protect them from the
enemy, Lord, but I also pray that You would protect them
from accidents. Guard them from such problems as friendly
fire or equipment failure.

I understand that no battlefield is safe, but I pray that Your
divine protection would follow our troops and hedge them
round about. Please, Lord, let them never be injured or killed
because of anything that can be prevented, and help them
keep sharp minds in anticipating trouble. Lord, I pray that
miscommunication or mistakes would never cost a life.

Lord, we commit our soldiers into Your care. Guard them
both in body and in mind and bring them home safely to
their families.

Amen.

BUT THOSE WHO WAIT ON THE LORD

shall renew their strength; they shall mount up
with wings like eagles, they shall run and
not be weary, they shall walk and not faint.

ISAIAH 40:31 (NKJV)

O GOD THE LORD,

the strength of my salvation,
you have covered my head in the day of battle.

PSALM 140:7 (NKJV)

*You gain strength, courage, and confidence
by every experience in which you stop
to look fear in the face. You must do
that which you think you cannot do.*

—ELEANOR ROOSEVELT

A PRAYER FOR STRENGTH FOR THE EXTRA MILE

FATHER GOD, bless the men and women of our Armed Forces with strength to do their duty. Lord, be their portion, their strength, and their provision. Bear them up when they are tired and renew their vigor, both mentally and physically.

Jesus, please encourage them when they are down and let their endurance be up to the tasks set before them. Let them be willing to help others, even when they are tired, and to go the extra mile with their fellow comrades. As Your Word says, let them "not become weary in doing good," and remind them that they will reap a harvest if they don't give up, as it says in Galatians 6:9.

Father, I ask that the members of our military get enough to eat of good and healthy food, and even in stressful situations, help their sleep refresh them and make them alert and able to press on.

Amen.

IF YOU HAD ONE HUNDRED SHEEP,
and one of them strayed away and was lost in the wilderness,
wouldn't you leave the ninety-nine others to go and search
for the lost one until you found it? And then you would
joyfully carry it home on your shoulders. When you arrived,
you would call together your friends and neighbors to
rejoice with you because your lost sheep was found.
In the same way, heaven will be happier over one lost sinner
who returns to God than over ninety-nine others
who are righteous and haven't strayed away!

Luke 15:4-7 (nlt)

'WHAT WILL A WOMAN DO if she
has ten silver coins and loses one of them? Won't she
light a lamp, sweep the floor, and look carefully until she
finds it? Then she will call in her friends and neighbors
and say, "Let's celebrate! I've found the coin I lost."'
Jesus said, 'In the same way God's angels are happy
when even one person turns to him.'

Luke 15:8-10 (cev)

No one is home until everyone is home.

—UNKNOWN

28

A Prayer for POWs and MIAs

FATHER, I pray for those who have been taken captive in war. Give them the courage to persevere and also the knowledge that they have not been forgotten. May our nation find ways to rescue them safely and quickly. Guide our political negotiators in their efforts to gain the freedom of these courageous people.

I pray that they will not be used as pawns to the advantage of our enemies.

When their freedom is restored, let our POWs walk with pride and dignity because of the suffering they have endured.

I ask for that more efficient ways of tracing and identifying those who are missing in action. Let them not be forgotten, fill them with the hope of freedom and the knowledge that their loved ones and comrades anxiously await their return.

Lord, I pray that You give each missing soldier courage and strength to persevere. Give them peace in knowing You'll never leave them. I pray that You clear their minds of any worry or anxiety so they may focus on finding their way to safety.

Lord, I pray and believe You will bring each soldier back to safety.

Amen.

TRUST IN HIM AT ALL TIMES,
you people; pour out your heart before Him;
God is a refuge for us. Selah

Psalm 62:8

AND I WILL PRAY THE FATHER,
and he shall give you another Comforter, that he may abide
with you for ever; Even the Spirit of truth; whom the world
cannot receive, because it seeth him not, neither knoweth
him: but ye know him; for he dwelleth with you,
and shall be in you. I will not leave you comfortless.

John 14:16-18 (KJV)

*I pray that our Heavenly Father may
assuage the anguish of your bereavement
and leave you only the cherished memory
of the loved and lost and the solemn pride
that must be yours to have laid so costly
a sacrifice upon the altar of freedom.*

—ABRAHAM LINCOLN

A Prayer of Comfort for Loved Ones

FATHER, I pray for the families of our military before You. Bless them for the sacrifices they make in service to this nation. Help them cope with the stress and special challenges that are common to military families. Give them hope in times of despair. Give them courage when faced with fears. Give them faith in times of doubt and uncertainty. Send ministers, friends, and other families across their paths to encourage and support them during tough times.

I ask You to give spouses the strength to endure the hardships of household management and assume responsibilities of mother and father during times of separation. If it is necessary to move, help spouses and children adjust to new communities, new schools, and quickly make new friends.

May Your peace that passes all understanding reside in their hearts and homes. May all their needs be met so that they have no lack. May Your blessings be upon them in every area of their lives. Comfort them by Your Spirit and Word that they might have faith to see their sons and daughters, husbands and wives returned to them safely. I pray You reveal Yourself to them and that they turn to Your Word for hope, peace, and encouragement.

Amen.

TWO PEOPLE CAN ACCOMPLISH more than
twice as much as one; they get a better return for their labor.
If one person falls, the other can reach out and help.
But people who are alone when they fall are in real trouble.
And on a cold night, two under the same blanket can gain
warmth from each other. But how can one be warm alone?
A person standing alone can be attacked and defeated,
but two can stand back-to-back and conquer. Three are
even better, for a triple-braided cord is not easily broken.

ECCLESIASTES 4:9-12 (NLT)

AND WHOEVER COMPELS YOU
to go one mile, go with him two.

MATTHEW 5:41 (NKJV)

We have learned that we cannot live alone,
at peace; that our own well-being is dependent
on the well-being of other nations, far away.
We have learned that we must live as men,
and not as ostriches, nor as dogs in the manger.
We have learned to be citizens of the world,
members of the human community.

—FRANKLIN DELANO ROOSEVELT

A PRAYER FOR OUR ALLIES

HEAVENLY FATHER, I thank You for the nations that ally themselves with the United States. Thank You for the countries that support the United States. Lord, I pray that You would bless them for faithfulness; cause the people of our nation to be good representatives of You to them.

Help us to always stay true to what is right. Lord, especially bless our ally Israel. We pray and ask You for the peace of Jerusalem.

Lord, let our policies always be right in Your sight, and let us lead righteously in the world community. Help America to set high standards for every form of belief and conduct for the world, starting with those nations allied to us and with whom we must interact.

I ask that America never sacrifice principle in order to make friends or allies of other nations. Help us to maintain a godly national sovereignty and not be deluded by the beliefs of nations that don't reverence You.

Amen.

I LOVE YOU, LORD! You answered my prayers. You paid attention to me, and so I will pray to you as long as I live. Death attacked from all sides, and I was captured by its painful chains. But when I was really hurting, I prayed and said, 'Lord, please don't let me die!' You are kind, Lord, so good and merciful. You protect ordinary people, and when I was helpless, you saved me and treated me so kindly that I don't need to worry anymore.

PSALM 116:1-7 (CEV)

THESE ARE THE ONES coming out of the great tribulation. They washed their robes in the blood of the Lamb and made them white. That is why they are standing in front of the throne of God, serving him day and night in his Temple. And he who sits on the throne will live among them and shelter them. They will never again be hungry or thirsty, and they will be fully protected from the scorching noontime heat. For the Lamb who stands in front of the throne will be their Shepherd. He will lead them to the springs of life-giving water. And God will wipe away all their tears.

REVELATION 7:14-17 (NLT)

This nation fights reluctantly, because we know the cost, and we dread the days of mourning that always come.

—GEORGE W. BUSH

A PRAYER OF COMFORT FOR SURVIVORS

DEAR HEAVENLY FATHER, please console those who have survived the death of loved ones and give them comfort in their lonely times. Be with them always, Lord, and let them feel Your presence as they cope with the passing of someone they loved.

Bless the families who are left without fathers or mothers, brothers and sisters, husbands or wives. Your Word tells us that You have sent to us the Comforter, Your Holy Spirit, to be with us, and I pray that Your Spirit would attend these families that have suffered loss.

Lord, also bless the comrades of those who have fallen. Heal the emotional damage of lost friendships. Help those who survive to go on with their duties and to quickly deal with the loss of their friends.

Lord, please ensure that those, whose time has come, have opportunities to meet You before the end of their lives. Help them be in right relationship with You when they meet You for eternity.

Amen.

THE LORD SAYS, 'I will rescue those who
love me. I will protect those who trust in my name.
When they call on me, I will answer; I will be with them
in trouble. I will rescue them and honor them. I will
satisfy them with a long life and give them my salvation.'

PSALM 91:14-16 (NLT)

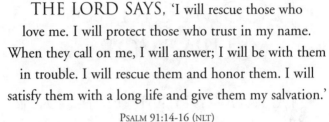

BUT LET ALL WHO TAKE REFUGE
in you be glad; let them ever sing for joy.
Spread your protection over them, that those
who love your name may rejoice in you.

PSALM 5:11

*If war is forced upon us, we will fight in
a just cause and by just means, sparing,
in every way we can, the innocent. And as
we and our coalition partners are doing in
Afghanistan, we will bring to the Iraqi people
food and medicines and supplies and freedom.*

—GEORGE W. BUSH

A PRAYER OF PROTECTION FOR CIVILIANS

HEAVENLY FATHER, I recognize that our world is not always peaceful and that brave men and women must defend what is right, putting their lives in jeopardy to defend their families and nations; but Lord, please bless and protect the innocent on both sides of every conflict. Let them remain safe despite fighting, let weapons aimed at military targets never miss their mark, and never permit civilians to be the targets of military action.

I ask You, to be the shield and defender of all of those who cannot defend themselves. It says in the Bible that vengeance is Yours, O Lord, and I pray that You would avenge innocent people who are purposefully targeted for violence and terrorism. Cause those people who target civilians to have a deep and meaningful change of heart and tactics.

Help the men and women of our military to uphold the highest moral and ethical standards as they prosecute war, and help them to show the same respect to the civilians of our enemies as they would have shown to their own families.

Amen.

PRAYERS FOR THE NATION

Grant us brotherhood in hope and union,
not only for the space of this bitter way,
but for the days to come which shall
and must unite all the children of earth.

—FRANKLIN DELANO ROOSEVELT

I URGE, then, first of all, that requests, prayers, intercession and thanksgiving be made for everyone— for kings and all those in authority, that we may live peaceful and quiet lives in all godliness and holiness.

1 TIMOTHY 2:1,2

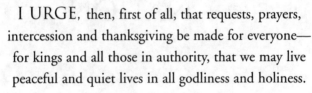

THE KING'S HEART is in the hand of the LORD; he directs it like a watercourse wherever he pleases.

PROVERBS 21:1

Leaders are visionaries with a poorly developed sense of fear and no concept of the odds against them. They make the impossible happen.

—ROBERT JARVIK

A PRAYER FOR OUR PRESIDENT

DEAR FATHER, in the name of Jesus, I pray for the President of the United States of America.

I know that his heart is in Your hand, so I ask You to guide him as the Commander-in-Chief of our nation.

Surround our president with wise counsel—men and women of integrity who place the good of this nation above their own, and whose motives are pure, honest, and trustworthy. Give our president discernment, understanding, and knowledge. Strengthen him spiritually, mentally, and physically. Give him courage and fortitude to stand strong in the face of adversity. Grant him boldness to lead our nation with integrity and honor.

I pray for the safety and protection of the president and his family. Give them strength to deal with the pressures of being the first family.

Thank You for working in and through the leadership of our president, so that we might lead peaceable lives in godliness and honesty.

Amen.

I WILL LIE DOWN and sleep in peace,
for you alone, O LORD, make me dwell in safety.

PSALM 4:8

I MAY WALK THROUGH VALLEYS
as dark as death, but I won't be afraid. You are with me,
and your shepherd's rod makes me feel safe.
You treat me to a feast, while my enemies watch.

PSALM 23:4,5 (CEV)

*Terrorist attacks can shake the foundations
of our biggest buildings, but they
cannot touch the foundation of America.
These acts shatter steel, but they cannot
dent the steel of American resolve.*

—UNKNOWN

PROTECTION
FROM TERRORISM

FATHER, in the name of the Lord Jesus, I pray that You prevent the destructive forces of terrorism directed against our nation. Provide protection from evil attacks and stop the aggressors who attempt to bring destruction to our nation and people.

I pray against the spirit of fear that accompanies the cowardice acts of terrorism. Allow our fear to turn to trust in You. May knowledge of terrorist planned attacks be revealed to those who provide our national and international security.

Provide strength, courage, and wisdom to the protectors of this nation to administer their duties. Give wisdom and insight to our government and everyone involved in the elimination of terrorism. Provide instruction in the development of effective and efficient anti-terrorist strategies that will give us an advantage against our aggressors.

I pray that the instigators of terrorism recognize the evil of their ways, and repent and denounce their cowardice acts of destruction against humanity.

Guide us in efforts to seek out and eradicate these merchants of death. Reveal the names of those responsible and in allegiance with terrorist organizations to our authorities.

Lord, help us to understand lifestyle changes that might be necessary to ensure our protection. Grant patience and tolerance to us in adapting to the safety precautions and measures that we might experience. Enable us to realize that the cost of inconvenience is a small price to pay for the safety of our families and of our nation.

Amen.

THE SLOTHFUL BECOME

impoverished, but the diligent gain wealth.

PROVERBS 11:16

WHEN YOU BECOME SUCCESSFUL,

don't say, 'I'm rich, and I've earned it all myself.'
Instead, remember that the Lord your God gives
you the strength to make a living. That's how he
keeps the promise he made to your ancestors.

DEUTERONOMY 8:17,18 (CEV)

*We will work for a prosperity
that is broadly shared.*

—GEORGE W. BUSH

A Prayer for the Economy

L ORD, I thank You for the incredible prosperity with
which You have blessed this nation. Thank You that we
are a giving country and that we feed uncounted
numbers of people outside our own borders.

I know that we are to walk by faith and not sight and that You
care for the flowers of the field and the birds of the air, but
sometimes we encounter times when Your additional blessing
is welcome. Lord, in times of economic hardship, I pray that
You provide jobs for those who need them. I pray that You
would encourage investors to invest wisely, and cause new
sources of economic stimulation to provide upturns to keep
our country growing at a healthy rate with jobs for people
who desire to provide for themselves and their families.

Lord, help us to not make foolish financial decisions both on
an individual level and as a nation, and give our leaders the
ability to make smart choices for this country's economic
growth. Thank You that You are our provider, Lord, and not
the federal government or even our jobs!

Amen.

THE AUTHORITIES ARE SENT BY GOD

to help you. But if you are doing something wrong,
of course you should be afraid, for you will
be punished. The authorities are established by God
for that very purpose, to punish those who do wrong.

ROMANS 13:4 (NLT)

THERE IS NO NEED to be afraid of the authorities.

Just do right, and they will praise you for it. After all, they
are God's servants, and it is their duty to help you. If you do
something wrong, you ought to be afraid, because these rulers
have the right to punish you. They are God's servants who
punish criminals to show how angry God is. But you should
obey the rulers because you know it is the right thing to do,
and not just because of God's anger. You must also pay
your taxes. The authorities are God's servants, and it is their
duty to take care of these matters. Pay all that you owe,
whether it is taxes and fees or respect and honor.

ROMANS 13:3-7 (CEV)

*In the time we have it is surely our duty
to do all the good we can to all the people
we can in all the ways we can.*

—WILLIAM BARCLAY

A PRAYER FOR
LAW ENFORCEMENT OFFICERS, FIREFIGHTERS, AND PARAMEDICS

FATHER, thank You for those people who daily put their lives in danger in our cities to protect us from crime, save us from danger, and treat us in emergency situations. I pray that You would bless and reward them for their service.

Lord, prosper and protect our law enforcement officers—give them wisdom to prevent crime and apprehend those who perpetrate it. Let them be people of integrity and preserve them from corruption and danger.

Bless our firefighters, Lord, and keep them safe as they deal with the hostile forces of nature. Help them to use godly insight in dealing with fires and other troubles, preserving life and property to the extent of their ability.

Be with our paramedics and other emergency responders. Thank You for these selfless helpers who strive daily to stand in the way of death. Help them to treat our injuries with extreme insight and grace, giving aid to those in such desperate need.

Thank You, Lord, for these volunteers on the front lines, and help those of us not exposed to the gritty nature of crime, destruction, and death to be as servant-minded as these people who protect and care for us. Help us to always keep them and their efforts in our prayers.

Amen.

IF MY PEOPLE, who are called by my name,
will humble themselves and pray and seek
my face and turn from their wicked ways,
then will I hear from heaven and will
forgive their sin and will heal their land.

2 Chronicles 7

Honest conviction is my courage . . .
—ANDREW JACKSON

*Our great resources . . . are more especially to
be found in the virtue, patriotism and
intelligence of our fellow-citizens.*
—JAMES MONROE

A PRAYER FOR NATIONAL PATRIOTISM

FATHER, In the name of Jesus, I ask that you would raise up, inside our hearts, an irrevocable sense of pride for this wonderful country in which we live. I pray that You would move us to attentively honor and support the precepts upon which this great nation was established.

Help us to never take for granted the freedoms that are afforded us, because we are citizens of the United States of America.

Show us ways to be excellent examples of patriotism to those around us, in both words and actions. And forgive us for the times, we may not have been the standard You would have desired.

Lord, remind us to be prayerful for the strength and preservation of America.

Fill our hearts with courage that we might be shining witnesses of Your standards, and counted noble patriots of this blessed nation—America—the land of the free and the home of the brave.

Amen.

A KINGDOM AT WAR
with itself will collapse.
A home divided against itself is doomed.

MARK 3:23 (NLT)

AS IRON SHARPENS IRON,
so a man sharpens the countenance of his friend.

PROVERBS 27:17 (NKJV)

*We must, indeed, all hang
together or, most assuredly,
we shall all hang separately.*

—BENJAMIN FRANKLIN

A PRAYER FOR UNITY AND COOPERATION

L ORD, I pray that You would inspire a spirit of cooperation and unity within our government. I thank You that our government was founded on a system of checks and balances, and that we have different political viewpoints that help to balance one another, but I pray that despite differences, the various parties and interest groups would be able to work together in agreement for the good of our nation.

I ask You to enable the various domestic agencies in charge of our civil defense to communicate effectively, and bless the integration of the Homeland Defense participants. Help them to protect our country from within while our Armed Forces protect us abroad.

Lord, help people to vote righteously, and cause our representatives at both state and national levels to work toward agreements that are good for our country and to make righteous decisions. Foster unity and cooperation in our government, Lord.

Amen.

OBEY THE GOVERNMENT, for God is the one who put it there. All governments have been placed in power by God. So those who refuse to obey the laws of the land are refusing to obey God, and punishment will follow. For the authorities do not frighten people who are doing right, but they frighten those who do wrong. So do what they say, and you will get along well. The authorities are sent by God to help you. But if you are doing something wrong, of course you should be afraid, for you will be punished. The authorities are established by God for that very purpose, to punish those who do wrong. So you must obey the government for two reasons: to keep from being punished and to keep a clear conscience.

ROMANS 13:1-5 (NLT)

Those who expect to reap the
blessings of freedom must, like men,
undergo the fatigue of supporting it.
—THOMAS PAINE

A Prayer for Our Congress

HEAVENLY FATHER, I pray that You would bless the United States Congress. Bless each member of both the House of Representatives and the Senate, and guide these elected officials in their decisions, that they would make choices that are both good for America and holy in Your sight.

Thank You that they often pray and honor You, and I ask that You would strengthen their resolve to publicly acknowledge You. Aid them in representing the people they were elected to represent. Cause them to cast godly votes and to propose righteous legislation guided by Your dictates rather than fickle public opinion. Give them wisdom to accurately discern the issues presented before them. May they be fair and just, hearing out all reasonable voices.

Keep our politicians honest, Lord, and cause them to conduct their affairs honorably, ethically, and with integrity. Help them live upright and morally just lives. May Your Word be the foundation of their lives. Bring any who do not know You to salvation through Your Son.

Amen.

GO THEREFORE and make disciples of all the nations,
baptizing them in the name of the Father and of the
Son and of the Holy Spirit, teaching them to observe
all things that I have commanded you; and lo,
I am with you always, even to the end of the age.

MATTHEW 28:19,20 (NKJV)

ASK ME FOR THE NATIONS,
and every nation on earth will belong to you.

PSALM 2:8 (CEV)

For we must consider that
we shall be as a city on a hill.
The eyes of all people are upon us.

—JOHN WINTHROP

A PRAYER FOR FAVOR AMONG THE NATIONS

HEAVENLY FATHER, thank You for blessing our country for so many years. Lord, we give You the credit for the prosperity of our nation, and we ask You to continue to bless our country with favor among the other nations of the world.

You know that America has unselfishly offered aid to countless people and many countries over the years, and sometimes it seems as though we often stand alone. Lord, help other nations share the deep convictions that still reside within this country's core of believers and to follow our lead of giving and watchfulness.

Lord, grant us allies who follow You. Help other countries to also support Israel and to promote the peace of Jerusalem and to reject all those who perpetrate terrorism. Thank You for the countries which have stood by us for so many years and that have fought with us for freedom.

Bless even those nations with which we have hostilities or have warred with, and draw them as a nation to a relationship with Your Son Jesus. Save our enemies, Lord, and grant our country favor with those who despise that for which we stand—You and freedom. Lord, break the ruling spirits over the nations that reject You and resist us because we are a Christian nation; draw those who don't know You in these countries to Yourself.

Amen.

AND HE HAS MADE from one blood every nation
of men to dwell on all the face of the earth, and has
determined their preappointed times and the boundaries
of their dwellings, so that they should seek the Lord,
in the hope that they might grope for Him and find Him.

ACTS 17:26,27 (NKJV)

A MAN WHO HAS FRIENDS
must himself be friendly, but there is
a friend who sticks closer than a brother.

PROVERBS 18:24 (NKJV)

All for one, one for all.

—ALEXANDER DUMAS

Prayer for National Unity

FATHER, I pray that You restore a social conscience to our nation. Thank You for the rich and glorious heritage we have as a country. Let us never forget that this was a country founded upon religious freedom and the principles and precepts of Your Word. May the same spirit reside in us as it did in our founding fathers. Let us never forget the thousands upon thousands who shed their blood and gave their lives so we might enjoy the freedoms we now have.

Help us unite together in support of our nation. Help us rise above political, racial, and social differences, to stand together as citizens of the United States of America. Let us bind together in support of our President, military, and Congress.

Help us be mindful to pray for our nation and its leaders. Lead us to pray for those in authority to make the right decisions that will keep our nation strong. Help us remember that even though our country may have faults, it deserves the loyalty, commitment, and support of all citizens.

Lord, this country was founded on freedoms, and we ask You to preserve ours, but we also pray that no dissenter with harmful intentions or ideas would have success in harming this nation. Make us all of one mind, Lord—a mind toward You.

Amen.

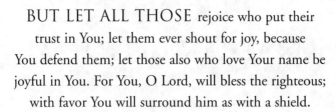

BUT LET ALL THOSE rejoice who put their
trust in You; let them ever shout for joy, because
You defend them; let those also who love Your name be
joyful in You. For You, O Lord, will bless the righteous;
with favor You will surround him as with a shield.

PSALM 5:11,12 (NKJV)

THE LORD SAYS, 'If you love me and truly
know who I am, I will rescue you and keep you safe.
When you are in trouble, call out to me. I will answer
and be there to protect and honor you. You will
live a long life and see my saving power.'

PSALM 91:14-16 (CEV)

*And let us not trust to human effort alone,
but humbly acknowledging the power and
goodness of Almighty God, who presides over the
destiny of nations, and who has at times been
revealed in our country's history; let us invoke
His aid and His blessings upon our labors.*

—GROVER CLEVELAND

A PRAYER FOR PROTECTION OF CIVILIANS ABROAD

HEAVENLY FATHER, we come before You to intercede for our land, the United States of America, and for the citizens who live abroad. We ask that You would keep our loved ones, friends, and leaders, safe within Your care during this time of upheaval and uncertainty.

We approach you with thankful hearts, realizing that Your love and Protection is without limit and boundary. We place our absolute trust in You as the one true Almighty God. We stand upon Your Word, in which You have promised to rescue and keep safe those who honor You.

Lord, we ask that You would bring a renewed hope and pride into the hearts of those who live outside the borders of our blessed nation. Protect them from terrorism, threat, or violence and help them to be proud representatives of America and courageous witnesses of You.

Amen.

THEN IF MY PEOPLE who are called by my name
will humble themselves and pray and seek my face and
turn from their wicked ways, I will hear from heaven
and will forgive their sins and heal their land.

2 CHRONICLES 7:14 (NLT)

SO TURN TO GOD! Give up your sins,
and you will be forgiven. Then that time will come
when the Lord will give you fresh strength.
He will send you Jesus, his chosen Messiah.

ACTS 3:19,20 (CEV)

*Whatever America hopes to bring to
pass in this world must first come
to pass in the heart of America.*

—DWIGHT D. EISENHOWER

A PRAYER FOR REPENTANCE

HEAVENLY FATHER, we come before You to intercede for our land, the United States of America. We come to You on behalf of our country, knowing that You have promised to answer the prayers of those who make requests of You.

Lord, forgive us for removing Your Commandments from our schools and making them places of violence instead of godly learning. Lord, forgive us for shutting You out of our workplaces. We ask You to replace the violence and isolation in our neighborhoods with brotherly love.

We thank You for the godly, moral foundation on which this nation was set, and we ask You to help us return to a place of right standing with You. Restore to us the peace and love You gave us in the beginning, which we've allowed to be overshadowed by secular values.

Help us to represent You in our daily lives and to take our faith outside the walls of our churches and into our schools, workplaces, and neighborhoods, showing the love of Christ. Redeem and protect our nation, we humbly pray.

Amen.

THROW OFF YOUR OLD evil nature and
your former way of life, which is rotten through and
through, full of lust and deception. Instead, there must
be a spiritual renewal of your thoughts and attitudes.

EPHESIANS 4:22,23 (NLT)

AND I WILL GIVE THEM singleness of heart
and put a new spirit within them. I will take away
their hearts of stone and give them tender hearts instead,
so they will obey my laws and regulations. Then they
will truly be my people, and I will be their God.

EZEKIEL 11:19,20 (NLT)

A great civilization is not
conquered from without until
it has destroyed itself within.

—WILL DURANT

62

A Prayer for Renewed Spiritual Vitality

HEAVENLY FATHER, I ask You to revive the Christians of our land—to breathe in us a renewed spiritual vitality. Our nation was once far more God-fearing than we are today, and our foundations were set on firm beliefs in You and Your precepts; Lord, draw us back to Yourself and to the immutable convictions that set this nation apart from any other in the world!

Lord, revive the Church as a corporate body. We have let our faith become nothing more than a religion, and I ask that You coax the failing coal of our belief into a burning flame once again. Our fire has burned dim, Lord, and we have become professionals and members of an institution rather than people earnestly seeking You together. Revive our churches, Lord! Break off the shackles of religion we place on ourselves!

Lord, help us to realize we should and can have an impact on our world! Help us to be bold for You, to witness with vitality, and to have a passion welling up from within that others will see and notice. Lord, help us to be proactive for You in our homes, our neighborhoods, our workplaces, our government, and our world.

Amen.

FOR GOD SO LOVED THE WORLD

that He gave His only begotten Son, that whoever
believes in Him should not perish but have everlasting life.
For God did not send His Son into the world to condemn
the world, but that the world through Him might be saved.

JOHN 3:16,17 (NKJV)

I ASSURE YOU, anyone who believes in me already
has eternal life. Yes, I am the bread of life! Your ancestors
ate manna in the wilderness, but they all died. However,
the bread from heaven gives eternal life to everyone
who eats it. I am the living bread that came down out
of heaven. Anyone who eats this bread will live forever;
this bread is my flesh, offered so the world may live.

JOHN 6:47-50

Amazing grace! How sweet the sound
That saved a wretch like me!
I once was lost, but now am found,
Was blind, but now I see.

—JOHN NEWTON

A PRAYER for SALVATION

DEAR LORD, I come before You to pray for my country. Your Word tells us that we can ask for the nations and that You'll give them to us; but right now I do not ask for the salvation of other nations—though we do want them to come to know You—I ask for the salvation of people within my own country.

Lord, God-fearing men and women seeking religious freedom founded the United States of America, but we have become a nation that seems to seek freedom *from* religion. We have departed so far from the vision with which this nation of free people was established, and we ask You to draw us back, both as a country and individually.

Woo those who have once known You and have strayed, and draw those who have never been presented with Your love into a relationship with You. I ask You for millions of souls, Lord! Let the people of America quit *claiming* to believe in You and begin truly *knowing* You!

Cause Christians to be bold for You, Lord, and help us to show Your love instead of presenting an attitude of judgment and condemnation to those who don't know You. You are love, Lord, and we want to be as You are. Help us show Your love.

Amen.

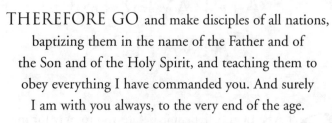

THEREFORE GO and make disciples of all nations,
baptizing them in the name of the Father and of
the Son and of the Holy Spirit, and teaching them to
obey everything I have commanded you. And surely
I am with you always, to the very end of the age.

MATTHEW 28:19,20

GO INTO ALL THE WORLD and preach
the Good News to everyone, everywhere. Anyone who
believes and is baptized will be saved. But anyone who refuses
to believe will be condemned. These signs will accompany
those who believe: They will cast out demons in my name,
and they will speak new languages…. They will be
able to place their hands on the sick and heal them.

MARK 16:15-18 (NLT)

Go, tell it on the mountain,
Over the hills and eve'rywhere;
Go, tell it on the mountain
That Jesus Christ is born!

—JOHN W. WORK, JR.

A Prayer About
Sharing the Gospel

DEAR LORD JESUS, I come before You to ask
for a renewed passion for sharing Your Gospel with
the whole world. Lord, the Great Commission tells us
to take Jesus to the world, and I admit that I have been preoc-
cupied with my own life. Lord, make me an effective witness
for You.

Jesus, cause my life to mirror You—reflecting You more
clearly in my actions each day. Help my very life be a testimony to Your greatness and ability to redeem any life and
any situation. Lord, cause my attitudes and reactions to be
Christ-like; help me be a good representative for You here on
earth—Your hands and feet.

Father, help me to be more bold in sharing the revelation
You have put in my heart. Help my words match my actions
and deeds, and make me open to the move of Your Holy
Spirit in me, telling me what to say in the situations where I
should share You but in my own flesh don't know what to
say. Put the words on my lips, Lord, and give me boldness to
proclaim You!

Amen.

PERSONAL PRAYERS

I hope I shall possess firmness and virtue enough to maintain what I consider the most enviable of all titles, the character of an honest man.

—GEORGE WASHINGTON

DRAW NEAR TO GOD

and he will draw near to you.

JAMES 4:8 (NKJV)

YES, everything else is worthless when compared
with the priceless gain of knowing Christ Jesus
my Lord. I have discarded everything else, counting
it all as garbage, so that I may have Christ.

PHILIPPIANS 3:8 (NLT)

*I searched for God
until He found me.*

—BLAISE PASCAL

A Prayer on Drawing Closer to God

DEAR HEAVENLY FATHER, as my country goes to war and enters a period of uncertainty, I pray that You will help me make this an opportunity to grow closer to You. God, You know that I have a measure of faith, but I pray that You would help my faith to grow even stronger and greater.

When life seems trouble-free and comfortable, it is easy for me to believe somehow that I have things under control and don't need Your help quite as much—that doesn't help me grow. And I don't want to be a person of weak faith, so use this hard time to draw me closer to You.

Today I want to know You more intimately, and knowing You desire this of me, I confess my absolute dependence on You. I declare that nothing I possess, any accomplishment, or ability can compare to the privilege and joy of knowing You. I thank You right now that You are strengthening me in my faith.

Amen.

DEVOTE YOURSELVES TO PRAYER
with an alert mind and a thankful heart.

COLOSSIANS 4:2

REJOICE IN THE LORD ALWAYS.
I will say it again: Rejoice! Do not be anxious about anything, but in everything, by prayer and petition, with thanksgiving, present your requests to God.

PHILIPPIANS 4:4,6

ENTER INTO HIS GATES with thanksgiving,
and into His courts with praise. Be thankful to Him, and bless His name. For the Lord is good; His mercy is everlasting, and His truth endures to all generations.

PSALM 100:4,5 (NKJV)

My country gave me schooling, independence of action, and opportunity for service. I am indebted to my country beyond any human power to repay.

—HERBERT HOOVER

A Prayer on Being Thankful for My Country

DEAR LORD, You are a good, kind, faithful, loving God. Your mercies are new every morning. You give us strength to handle every challenge that we face. You are the Giver of all good gifts and blessings.

One of the greatest blessings in my life is the country in which I live. When I look at all the nations of the world, I realize anew that it is a country of prosperity and generosity, of strength and safety, of opportunity and work, of law and grace.

Your hand has been on this land since its inception. And I know that Your hand will be on my country in this time of war. I pray that You will renew in my heart a sense of gratitude for this great nation. Help me to never take my country for granted or to ignore any of Your other blessings on my life.

Today I come into Your presence with thanksgiving and praise. I rejoice in You. I declare Your faithfulness. And I thank You that You have blessed me so much to be a citizen of this land.

Amen.

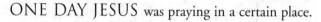

ONE DAY JESUS was praying in a certain place. When he finished, one of his disciples said to him, 'Lord, teach us to pray, just as John taught his disciples.' He said to them, 'When you pray, say: "Father, hallowed be your name, your kingdom come. Give us each day our daily bread. Forgive us our sins, for we also forgive everyone who sins against us. And lead us not into temptation."'

LUKE 11:1-4

PRAY AT ALL TIMES and on every occasion in the power of the Holy Spirit. Stay alert and be persistent in your prayers for all Christians everywhere.

EPHESIANS 6:18 (NLT)

Prayer is of transcendent importance. Prayer is the mightiest agent to advance God's work. Praying hearts and hands only can do God's work. Prayer succeeds when all else fails.

—E.M. BOUNDS

A Prayer on Becoming a Prayer Warrior

D EAR GOD, what an incredible privilege, what an honor, what a personal blessing it is that You have invited me to come into Your very Presence through prayer! Forgive me for the times when I have not prayed to You because I thought I was too busy or because I simply didn't have the faith to believe that prayer changes the world—and changes me.

God, I acknowledge that I need to pray for my spiritual well being and for the various needs in my life. God, I also know I have friends and family who need my prayers. God, there is a lost and hurting world, which needs me to be a prayer warrior.

As my country is at war, I recommit myself right now to being a person of prayer. I will pray alone and with others. I will pray morning, noon, and night. I will voice words to You and I will be silent to listen for Your voice. Thank You that I will more and more become the person You want me to be through Your gracious invitation to talk with You each day.

Amen.

BE AN EXAMPLE TO ALL BELIEVERS
in what you teach, in the way you live,
in your love, your faith, and your purity.

1 TIMOTHY 4:12 (NLT)

AND YOU YOURSELF must be an example to them
by doing good deeds of every kind. Let everything you
do reflect the integrity and seriousness of your teaching.
Let your teaching be so correct that it can't be criticized.
Then those who want to argue will be ashamed because
they won't have anything bad to say about us.

TITUS 2:7,8 (NLT)

Do not let your deeds belie your words,
lest when you speak in church someone
may say to himself, 'Why do you not
practice what you preach?'

—ST. JEROME

A Prayer on Being an Example of Faith and Integrity

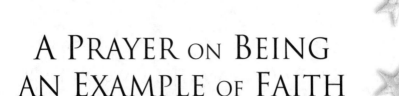

D EAR LORD, You have called people who know You to be examples of faith, purity, and integrity. We show to the world the nature and power of the Gospel through the way we live our lives.

Lord, I want to be a person who honors Your name in the way I live. Please protect me from temptation and evil ways. Help me to be free from a lifestyle of sin that would damage the cause of the Gospel in an unbeliever's eyes. Instead, Lord, let me exhibit qualities of grace, godly passion and enthusiasm, joyfulness, gratitude, gentleness, wisdom, generosity, honesty, kindness, faithfulness, and all the other fruit of the Spirit, which demonstrate to a skeptical world just how wonderful it is to know You.

In this time of war, people everywhere are looking for hope and truth. May my life be an example of Your power and grace.

Amen.

BUT HOW CAN THEY CALL ON HIM

to save them unless they believe in him? And how can
they believe in him if they have never heard about him?
And how can they hear about him unless someone
tells them? And how will anyone go and tell them without
being sent? That is what the Scriptures mean when they say,
'How beautiful are the feet of those who bring good news!'

ROMANS 10:15

FOR I AM NOT ASHAMED

of this Good News about Christ. It is the
power of God at work, saving everyone
who believes—Jews first and also Gentiles.

ROMANS 1:17 (NLT)

I'll tell the world how Jesus saved me,
And how He gave me a life brand new;
And I know that if you trust Him
That all He gave me
He'll give to you.

—BAYNARD L. FOX

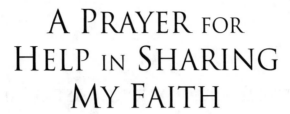

A Prayer for Help in Sharing My Faith

DEAR HEAVENLY FATHER, You are kind and gracious and slow to anger. Even when we have sinned and rebelled against You, Your desire is not to condemn us but to save us through Your Son Jesus Christ. You love us so much that even though we have acted as Your enemy, You sent Jesus to die for our sins.

Lord, thank You for the amazing love that is alive in my own life. And I pray, dear God, that I will never be satisfied to just experience Your love for myself, but will pass that love on to others.

God, in this time of war, there is so much uncertainty and fear. Millions of people who don't normally think about spiritual matters are searching for answers. You have put some of those people in my path. Would You give me the sensitivity to know who is ready to hear about Your grace and salvation? Would You give me the words to explain how to be saved? Would You create the opportunities for spiritual conversation and prayer to take place? Let Your Holy Spirit speak through me, showing Your love to those who do not know You.

God, I am not ashamed of Your Gospel or to tell the world of Your goodness!

Amen.

THEREFORE I EXHORT FIRST OF ALL
that supplications, prayers, intercessions, and giving of
thanks be made for all men, for kings and all who are
in authority, that we may lead a quiet and peaceable life
in all godliness and reverence. For this is good and acceptable
in the sight of God our Savior, who desires all men to
be saved and to come to the knowledge of the truth.

1 TIMOTHY 2:1-3 (NKJV)

THE LORD CONTROLS RULERS,
just as he determines the course of rivers.

PROVERBS 21:1 (CEV)

Live pure, speak true, right wrong,
follow the King—
Else, wherefore born?

—ALFRED, LORD TENNYSON

A PRAYER OF SUPPORT FOR MY LEADERS

ALMIGHTY GOD, You provide guidance, protection, and order in our world through leaders. Not all authority figures live according to Your will and ways—and You tell us that our first obedience and allegiance is to You. Yet You call for us to submit to authorities.

Lord, I ask You to forgive me for the times when I am rebellious and resistant to those in leadership positions over me. I admit that sometimes I simply do not want to follow the lead of those in positions of authority and want my own way. Help me to have strong convictions and still submit when You call me to do so.

Mighty God, in this moment of war, our nation's leaders need our support and prayers more than ever. And You want to teach me the lesson of being a good follower. Help me to be a leader in my attitude toward the President, Congress, military, as well as leaders at every level of government and business. I will serve You as I serve my leaders.

Amen.

DEAR FRIENDS, do not believe everyone who claims to speak by the Spirit. You must test them to see if the spirit they have comes from God. For there are many false prophets in the world. This is the way to find out if they have the Spirit of God: If a prophet acknowledges that Jesus Christ became a human being, that person has the Spirit of God. If a prophet does not acknowledge Jesus, that person is not from God. Such a person has the spirit of the Antichrist. You have heard that he is going to come into the world, and he is already here.

1 JOHN 4:1-3 (NLT)

SOMETIMES FALSE PROPHETS spoke to the people of Israel. False teachers will also sneak in and speak harmful lies to you. But these teachers don't really belong to the Master who paid a great price for them, and they will quickly destroy themselves. Many people will follow their evil ways and cause others to tell lies about the true way. They will be greedy and cheat you with smooth talk. But long ago God decided to punish them, and God doesn't sleep.

2 PETER 2:1-3 (CEV)

The function of wisdom is discriminating between good and evil.

—CICERO

A PRAYER FOR SPIRITUAL DISCERNMENT

DEAR HEAVENLY FATHER, we live in a day of spiritual confusion. There are thousands of voices who claim to know truth and the way to peace, happiness, and eternal life. Many of these teachers do not know nor acknowledge that You are the way, the truth, and the life, and that only by coming to God through Jesus can we be saved.

In times of crisis, false teachers will prey on those who are not strong in their faith and who are not familiar with Your Word. I pray that You will raise up men and women who will boldly proclaim the truth of Jesus Christ. I pray that You will protect the innocent and gullible from the malicious ones posing as shepherds that try to steal the sheep from the Good Shepherd.

God, I pray that I will always be able to give a reason for the hope that lies within me. I pray that I will not be tossed back and forth by waves of false teaching. I pray that I will continue to grow in wisdom and faith; that I will be mature and complete, lacking in nothing of spiritual value. Give me discernment from Your Holy Spirit, that I can divide truth from error and always remain on track with You.

Amen.

YOU HAVE HEARD that it was said,
'Love your neighbor and hate your enemy.' But I tell you:
Love your enemies and pray for those who persecute
you, that you may be sons of your Father in heaven.

MATTHEW 5:43-45

BUT WHEN YOU ARE PRAYING,
first forgive anyone you are holding a grudge against,
so that your Father in heaven will forgive your sins, too.

MARK 11:25 (NLT)

FORGIVE US OUR DEBTS, as we also
have forgiven our debtors…. For if you forgive men
when they sin against you, your heavenly Father
will also forgive you. But if you do not forgive men
their sins, your Father will not forgive your sins.

MATTHEW 6:12,14,15

Only the brave know how to forgive.
…A coward never forgave;
it is not in his nature.

—LAURENCE STERNE

A Prayer on Loving and Forgiving My Enemies

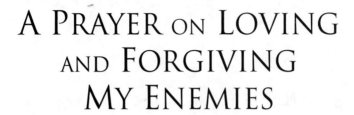

HEAVENLY FATHER, with my nation at war, it is very clear who my enemies are. And yet, You want me to love, forgive, and pray for these people—even the leaders who we believe created the circumstances of this war. You love each and every person on both sides of this war.

Father, just as former enemies have become close allies after previous wars in our nation's history, may the day come when there is reconciliation between our nations. May there be a mighty moving of your Spirit across the land of our foes, drawing millions to a saving knowledge of Jesus Christ.

Father, may our leaders, our soldiers, our citizens, and, most of all, may I exhibit a supernatural spirit of kindness and forgiveness. May we even help rebuild the nation we once fought and show on a national level the power of faith and love.

I want to be able to love everybody I encounter—even those who have shown themselves to be my enemy.

Amen.

MY FRIENDS, be glad, even if you have a lot of trouble. You know that you learn to endure by having your faith tested. But you must learn to endure everything, so that you will be completely mature and not lacking in anything.

JAMES 1:2-4 (CEV)

SO, if you think you are standing firm, be careful that you don't fall! No temptation has seized you except what is common to man. And God is faithful; he will not let you be tempted beyond what you can bear. But when you are tempted, he will also provide a way out so that you can stand up under it.

1 CORINTHIANS 10:12,13

Character, not circumstances, make the man.

—BOOKER T. WASHINGTON

A Prayer for Courage to Face Adversity

GRACIOUS GOD, when life becomes difficult, I find it easy to complain, feel sorry for myself, and even quit. I have it so good so often that I am not as prepared to resist the enemy effectively or maintain my Christian testimony as I should be.

I pray that I will always be mindful of the great love You have shown me through the sacrifice of Jesus Christ, who overcame all forms of suffering and temptation and yet still had all of my same human attributes. Lord, Jesus endured all the same temptations I endure, and yet He took the ways out You provided; Jesus also dealt with adversity constantly throughout His earthly ministry, and yet He remained the embodiment of Your ways and character.

Father, help me to mirror Your Son both in my behavior and in my heart. Help me to face the dark days and the bright with the same inner conviction that You are in control. Lord, help me take the escape routes from temptation that You provide. Jesus, help me love You more than I love sin or my old behaviors.

Thank You for giving me the help and strength I need to cope with temptation and adversity.

Amen.

TREMBLING WITH FEAR, the jailer called
for lights and ran to the dungeon and fell down before
Paul and Silas. He brought them out and asked, 'Sirs,
what must I do to be saved?' They replied, 'Believe on the
Lord Jesus and you will be saved, along with your entire
household.' Then they shared the word of the Lord with him
and all who lived in his household. That same hour the jailer
washed their wounds, and he and everyone in his household
were immediately baptized. Then he brought them into
his house and set a meal before them. He and his entire
household rejoiced because they all believed in God.

ACTS 16:29-34 (NLT)

NOW A CERTAIN woman named Lydia heard us. She
was a seller of purple from the city of Thyatira, who worshiped
God. The Lord opened her heart to heed the things spoken
by Paul. And when she and her household were baptized, she
begged us, saying, 'If you have judged me to be faithful to
the Lord, come to my house and stay.' So she persuaded us.

ACTS 16:14,15 (NKJV)

O give us homes built firm upon the Savior,
Where Christ is Head and Counselor and Guide;
Where ev'ry child is taught His love and favor
And gives his heart to Christ, the Crucified.

—BARBARA B. HART

A PRAYER FOR SALVATION FOR MY FAMILY

L OVING FATHER WHO SAVES, as I have prayed for my country—its leaders, its soldiers, its citizenry—I am reminded that You desire all to come to salvation, and I pray in particular for my family. Lord, how can I spread Your love amid the people of the world when I have so often failed to do so within my own family?

I pray right now that You would touch the heart of every member of my family who does not know Jesus Christ as their Lord and Savior. Please send people who know You to cross their paths and remind them of Your great love. Speak directly to their spirit through the Holy Spirit, who convicts of truth and sin.

Make my words effective when I speak to them. Provide me with opportunities to share the love You have planted in my heart. I pray that I will truly demonstrate the grace and love of a follower of Jesus Christ through my actions and that everyone in my family would come to know You.

Amen.

GREAT CREEDS, THOUGHTS, QUOTES, and PRAYERS

A PATRIOTIC CREED

To serve my country day by day
At any humble post I may;
To honor and respect her flag,
To live the traits of which I brag;
To be American in deed
As well as in my printed creed.

To stand for truth and honest toil,
To till my little patch of soil,
And keep in mind the debt I owe
To those who died that I might know
My country, prosperous and free,
And passed this heritage to me.

I always must in trouble's hour
Be guided by the men in power;
For God and country I must live,
My best for God and country give;
No act of mine that men may scan
Must shame the name "American."

To do my best and play my part,
American in mind and heart;
To serve the flag and bravely stand
To guard the glory of my land;
To be American in deed:
God grant me strength to keep this creed!

—EDGAR A. GUEST

STAND NOW

These are the times that try men's souls.
The summer soldier and the sunshine
patriot will, in this crisis, shrink from
the service of their country; but he
that stands it now, deserves the love
and thanks of man and woman.

—THOMAS PAINE

DIVINE HELP

In battle and in the face of danger and death,
he discloses those divine attributes which his
Maker gave when He created man in
His own image. No physical courage and
no brute instinct can take the place of the
Divine help which alone can sustain him.

—GENERAL DOUGLAS MACARTHUR

THE COST OF FREEDOM

The cost of freedom is always high,
but Americans have always paid it.
And one path we shall never choose,
and that is the path of surrender.

—JOHN F. KENNEDY

THE SOLDIER'S PSALM

D URING World War I, the 91st Infantry Brigade of the U.S. Expeditionary Army was preparing to enter combat in Europe. Most of the men were "green" soldiers, never having seen combat.

The commander, a devout Christian, called his men together and gave each a card on which was printed the 91st Psalm. He challenged them to recite aloud what he called the "Soldier's Psalm" daily.

The 91st Brigade was engaged in three of the bloodiest battles of World War I: Chateau Thierry, Belle Wood, and the Argonne.

While other American units similarly engaged experienced 90 percent casualty rates, the 91st Brigade did not suffer a single combat-related casualty!

PSALM 91
PERSONALIZED
for SOLDIERS

FATHER GOD, I thank You that I have chosen to dwell in Your secret place, and because I have done so, I remain stable and fixed under Your shadow. You are my God, my refuge and my fortress. On You I lean, rely, and confidently trust. I thank You that You deliver me from the snare of the fowler and from deadly pestilence. I thank You that You cover me with Your wings of protection, and under those wings I find a safe haven. Your truth and Your faithfulness are my shield and buckler.

Because of Your divine protection in my life, I am not afraid of the terror at night nor the evil plots and slanders of the wicked that fly by the day. I am not afraid of the pestilence that stalks in darkness. I am not afraid of destruction or calamity or sudden death that the enemy would attack me with.

A thousand may fall at my side and ten thousand at my right hand, but it shall not, will not, and cannot come near my family or me, because we are inaccessible in the secret place of the Most High.

Because I have made You, O Lord, my refuge and my dwelling place, no evil shall befall me. No plague or calamity shall come near my home or my family. You give Your angels charge over me to accompany, defend, and preserve me in all my ways. Wherever I go, whatever I do, Your angels go with me to protect me from harm, injury, and evil.

Even though I walk in the midst of danger and peril, it will have no effect on me. Because I have set my love on You, You will deliver me and set me on high. Because I have a personal knowledge of Your mercy, grace, and kindness, and because I trust and rely upon You, You will never forsake me. No, not ever. I will call upon You and You will answer me. You will be with me in time of trouble and You will deliver me and honor me with a long life. You satisfy me and show me Your salvation.

WHY PRAY?

THERE ARE THREE ways that men get what they
want: by planning, by working, and by praying.

Any great military operation takes careful planning. Then you
must have well-trained troops to carry it out—that's working.

But between the plan and the operation there is always an
unknown. That unknown spells defeat or victory, success or
failure. It is the reaction of the actors to the ordeal when it
actually comes. Some people call that getting the breaks; I call
it God.

God has His part, or margin, in everything. That's where
prayer comes in. Up to now, in the Third Army, God has
been very good to us. We have never retreated; we have suffered no defeats, no famine, no epidemics.

This is because a lot of people back home are praying for us.

GENERAL GEORGE S. PATTON, JR.
France, December 1944

THE MARINES'
HYMN

From the halls of Montezuma
To the shores of Tripoli,

We fight our country's battles
In the air, on land, and sea.

First to fight for right and freedom,
And to keep our honor clean,

We are proud to claim the title
Of United States Marines.

Our flag's unfurl'd to every breeze
From dawn to setting sun;

We have fought in every clime and place
Where we could take a gun.

In the snow of far-off northern lands
And in sunny tropic scenes,

You will find us always on the job—
The United States Marines.

Here's health to you and to our Corps
Which we are proud to serve;

In many a strife we've fought for life
And never lost our nerve.

If the Army and the Navy
Ever gaze on Heaven's scenes,

They will find the streets are guarded
By United States Marines.

MARINES' PRAYER

ALMIGHTY FATHER, whose command is over all and whose love never fails, make me aware of Thy Presence and obedient to Thy will. Keep me true to my best self, guarding me against dishonesty in purpose and deed and helping me to live so that I can face my fellow Marines, my loved ones, and Thee without shame or fear. Protect my family.

Give me the will to do the work of a Marine and to accept my share of responsibilities with vigor and enthusiasm. Grant me the courage to be proficient in my daily performance. Keep me loyal and faithful to my superiors and to the duties my Country and the Marine Corps have entrusted to me. Help me to wear my uniform with dignity, and let it remind me daily of the traditions which I must uphold.

If I am inclined to doubt, steady my faith; if I am tempted, make me strong to resist; if I should miss the mark, give me courage to try again.

Guide me with the light of truth and grant me wisdom by which I may understand the answer to my prayer.

Navy Hymn

Eternal Father, strong to save,
Whose arm hath bound the restless wave,
Who bid'st the mighty Ocean deep
Its own appointed limits keep;
O hear us when we cry to thee,
for those in peril on the sea.

O Christ! Whose voice the waters heard
And hushed their raging at Thy Word,
Who walked'st on the foaming deep,
and calm amidst its rage didst sleep;
Oh hear us when we cry to Thee
For those in peril on the sea!

Most Holy Spirit! Who didst brood
Upon the chaos dark and rude,
And bid its angry tumult cease,
And give, for wild confusion, peace;
Oh, hear us when we cry to Thee
For those in peril on the sea!

O Trinity of love and power!
Our brethren shield in danger's hour;
From rock and tempest, fire and foe,
Protect them wheresoe'er they go;
Thus evermore shall rise to Thee,
Glad hymns of praise from land and sea.

A NAVY FLYER'S CREED

I AM A UNITED STATES NAVY FLYER. My countrymen built the best airplane in the world and entrusted it to me. They trained me to fly it. I will use it to the absolute limit of my power. With my fellow pilots, air crews, and deck crews, my plane and I will do anything necessary to carry out our tremendous responsibilities. I will always remember we are part of an unbeatable combat team—the United States Navy. When the going is fast and rough, I will not falter. I will be uncompromising in every blow I strike. I will be humble in victory. I am a United States Navy flyer. I have dedicated myself to my country, with its many millions of all races, colors, and creeds. They and their way of life are worthy of my greatest protective effort. I ask the help of God in making that effort great enough.

THE U.S. AIR FORCE HYMN

Lord, guard and guide the men who fly
Through the great spaces of the sky;
Be with them traversing the air
In darkening storms or sunshine fair

Thou who dost keep with tender might
The balanced birds in all their flight
Thou of the tempered winds be near
That, having Thee, they know no fear

Control their minds with instinct fit
What time, adventuring, they quit
The firm security of land;
Grant steadfast eye and skillful hand

Aloft in solitudes of space,
Uphold them with Thy saving grace.
O God, protect the men who fly
Through lonely ways beneath the sky.

AIR FORCE PRAYER

OUR HEAVENLY FATHER, whose loving care encompasses even the sparrow in its flight, guide and protect, we pray, the men who fly the uncharted spaces of the sky. Bless those who, through service in the Air Force, stand guard over the sacred trust of home and country.

Endow them with wisdom and understanding, that they may clearly see the path of duty and courageously devote them-selves in service to the nation they love. In the solitude of flight may the beauty of Thy greatness be revealed to each of them that they may pattern their lives after Thine.

Extend Thy strengthening presence to those who wait at home; and may they ever know Thy watchful care will keep safe the absent one.

Let Thy benediction be upon us, O God we pray. Lead us to carry on the trust left by our brothers, who gave with honor their lives in service of their country. May we find peace in the knowledge of our mission accomplished and their task completed through service for Thee,

Amen.

—GENERAL HOYT S. VANDENBERG

UNITED STATES ARMY HYMN
"GOD OF OUR FATHERS"

God of our fathers, whose almighty hand
Leads forth in beauty all the starry band
Of shining worlds in splendor through the skies
Our grateful songs before Thy throne arise.

Thy love divine hath led us in the past,
In this free land by Thee our lot is cast,
Be Thou our Ruler, Guardian, Guide and Stay,
Thy Word our law, Thy paths our chosen way.

From war's alarms, from deadly pestilence,
Be Thy strong arm our ever sure defense;
Thy true religion in our hearts increase,
Thy bounteous goodness nourish us in peace.

Refresh Thy people on their toilsome way,
Lead us from night to never ending day;
Fill all our lives with love and grace divine,
And glory, laud, and praise be ever Thine.

—DANIEL C. ROBERTS, 1888

MIDSHIPMAN'S PRAYER

ALMIGHTY GOD, whose way is in the sea, whose paths are in the great waters, whose command is over all, and whose love never faileth; let me be aware of Thy presence and obedient to Thy will. Keep me true to my best self, guarding me against dishonesty in purpose and in deed, and helping me so to live that I can stand unashamed and unafraid before my shipmates, my loved ones, and Thee. Protect those in whose love I live. Give me the will to do my best and to accept my share of responsibilities with a strong heart and a cheerful mind. Make me considerate of those entrusted to my leadership and faithful to the duties my country has entrusted in me. Let my uniform remind me daily of the traditions of the service of which I am a part. If I am inclined to doubt, steady my faith; if I am tempted, make me strong to resist; If I should miss the mark, give me courage to try again. Guide me with the light of truth and give me strength to faithfully serve Thee, now and always.

Amen.

No Despair

We must never despair; our situation has been compromising before; and it changed for the better; so I trust it will again. If difficulties arise, we must put forth new exertion and proportion our efforts to the exigencies of the times.

—GEORGE WASHINGTON

In war: resolution.
In defeat: defiance.
In victory: magnanimity.
In peace: good will.

—SIR WINSTON CHURCHILL

WHAT CAN YOU DO FOR YOUR COUNTRY?

Let the word go forth from this time and place, to friend and foe alike, that the torch has been passed to a new generation of Americans, born in this century, tempered by war, disciplined by a hard and bitter peace, proud of our ancient heritage, and unwilling to witness or permit the slow undoing of those human rights to which this nation has always been committed, and to which we are committed today at home and around the world. Let every nation know, whether it wishes us well or ill, that we shall pay any price, bear any burden, meet any hardship, support any friend, oppose any foe to assure the survival and the success of liberty.

—JOHN F. KENNEDY

A Time for War

THERE IS A TIME FOR EVERYTHING,
and a season for every activity under heaven:
a time to be born and a time to die, a time to plant
and a time to uproot, a time to kill and a time to heal,
a time to tear down and a time to build, a time to weep
and a time to laugh, a time to mourn and a time to dance,
a time to scatter stones and a time to gather them,
a time to embrace and a time to refrain, a time to search
and a time to give up, a time to keep and a time to
throw away, a time to tear and a time to mend, a time
to be silent and a time to speak, a time to love and
a time to hate, a time for war and a time for peace.

ECCLESIASTES 3:1-8

GIVE ME LIBERTY OR GIVE ME DEATH!

*It is in vain, sir, to extenuate the matter.
Gentlemen may cry, "Peace, peace"—but
there is no peace. The war is actually begun!
The next gale that sweeps from the north
will bring to our ears the clash of resounding
arms! Our brethren are already in the field!
Why stand we here idle? What is it that
gentlemen wish? What would they have?
Is life so dear, or peace so sweet, as to be
purchased at the price of chains and slavery?
Forbid it, Almighty God! I know not what
course others may take; but as for me,
give me liberty or give me death!*

—PATRICK HENRY

A Prayer
for Victory

GOD OF OUR FATHERS, who by land and sea has ever led us on to victory, please continue Your inspiring guidance in this the greatest of our conflicts.

Strengthen my soul so that the weakening instincts of self-preservation, which besets all of us in battle, shall not blind me to my duty, to my own manhood, to the glory of my calling, and to my responsibility to my fellow soldiers.

Grant our Armed Forces that disciplined valor and mutual confidence which insures success in war.

Let me not mourn for the men who have died fighting, but rather let me be glad that such heroes have lived.

If it be my lot to die, let me do so with courage and honor in a manner which will bring the greatest harm to the enemy; and please, O Lord, protect and guide those I shall leave behind.

Give us the victory, Lord.

—GENERAL G. S. PATTON

*Believe in yourself. You gain strength,
courage, and confidence by every
experience in which you stop to look
fear in the face. You must do that
which you think you cannot do.*

—ELEANOR ROOSEVELT

*And so my fellow Americans,
ask not what your country can do for you;
ask what you can do for your country.*

—JOHN F. KENNEDY

A PRAYER FOR CONVICTION

ALMIGHTY GOD, we are about to be committed to a task from which some of us will not return. We go willingly to this hazardous adventure because we believe that those concepts of human dignity, rights, and justice that Your Son expounded to the world, and which are respected in the government of our beloved country, are in peril of extinction from the earth. We are ready to sacrifice ourselves for our country and our God. We do not ask, individually, for our safe return. But we earnestly pray that You will help each of us to do his full duty. Permit none of us to fail a comrade in the fight. Above all, sustain us in our conviction in the justice and righteousness of our cause so that we may rise above all terror of the enemy and come to You, if called, in the humble pride of the good soldier and in the certainty of Your infinite mercy.

Amen.

—GENERAL DWIGHT D. EISENHOWER

THE COMMANDER-IN-CHIEF'S PRAYER

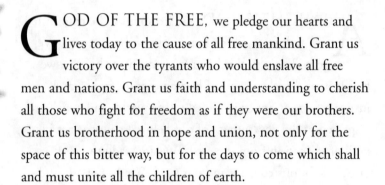

GOD OF THE FREE, we pledge our hearts and lives today to the cause of all free mankind. Grant us victory over the tyrants who would enslave all free men and nations. Grant us faith and understanding to cherish all those who fight for freedom as if they were our brothers. Grant us brotherhood in hope and union, not only for the space of this bitter way, but for the days to come which shall and must unite all the children of earth.

We are all of us children of earth. Grant us that simple knowledge. If our brothers are oppressed, then we are oppressed. If they hunger, we hunger. If their freedom is taken away, our freedom is not secure. Grant us a common faith that man shall know bread and peace—that he shall know justice and righteousness, freedom and security, an equal opportunity and an equal chance to do his best, not only in our own lands, but throughout the world. And in that faith let us march, toward the clean world our hands can make.

Amen.

—PRESIDENT FRANKLIN DELANO ROOSEVELT

A Prayer of Protection

ALMIGHTY GOD, we make our earnest prayer that Thou wilt keep the United States in Thy holy protection; that Thou wilt incline the hearts of the citizens to cultivate a spirit of subordination and obedience to government; to entertain a brotherly affection and love for one another and for their fellow-citizens of the United States at large.

Let us unite in imploring the Supreme Ruler of Nations to spread His holy protection over these United States to turn the machinations of the wicked; to the confirming of our Constitution; to enable us at all times to root out internal sedition and put invasion to flight; to perpetuate to our country that prosperity which His goodness has already conferred; and to verify the anticipations of this government being a safeguard of human rights.

Amen.

—PRESIDENT GEORGE WASHINGTON

GOD,
OUR REFUGE

GOD IS OUR REFUGE AND STRENGTH,
an ever-present help in trouble. Therefore we will not fear,
though the earth give way and the mountains fall into
the heart of the sea, though its waters roar and foam
and the mountains quake with their surging. *Selah*

There is a river whose streams make glad the city of God,
the holy place where the Most High dwells. God is within
her, she will not fall; God will help her at break of day.
Nations are in uproar, kingdoms fall; he lifts his voice,
the earth melts. The LORD Almighty is with us;
the God of Jacob is our fortress. *Selah*

PSALM 46:1-7

THE SPIRITUAL LIFE
OF THE SOLDIER

*I look upon the spiritual life of the soldier
as even more important than his physical
equipment. The soldier's heart, the soldier's
spirit, the soldier's soul are everything.
Unless the solder's soul sustains him, he
cannot be relied upon and will fail himself,
his commander, and his country in the end.
It's morale, and I mean morale, which wins
the victory in the ultimate, and that type of
morale can only come out of the religious
fervor in his soul. I count heavily on
that type of man and that kind of army.*

—GENERAL GEORGE C. MARSHALL

A 31-DAY
DEVOTIONAL

*Moments of crisis, perhaps none greater than war,
remind us of the absolute necessity of prayer.*

*How is your prayer life? Do you delight in spending time in
God's Presence? Do you present your petitions to Him with a
sense of excitement and anticipation? When war has passed
and life becomes just a bit more normal, will you still
approach your prayer life with the same spirit of urgency?*

*The following 31-day devotional, with excerpts from s
ome of the greatest writing on prayer ever penned, will
encourage you to become a man or woman of God devoted
to the great privilege and responsibility of intercession.*

DAY 1
WE MUST PRAY

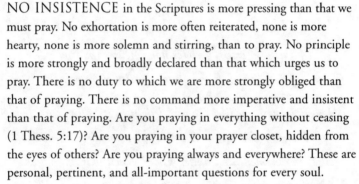

Don't worry about anything; instead, pray about everything.
Tell God what you need, and thank him for all he has done.

PHILIPPIANS 4:6 (NLT)

NO INSISTENCE in the Scriptures is more pressing than that we must pray. No exhortation is more often reiterated, none is more hearty, none is more solemn and stirring, than to pray. No principle is more strongly and broadly declared than that which urges us to pray. There is no duty to which we are more strongly obliged than that of praying. There is no command more imperative and insistent than that of praying. Are you praying in everything without ceasing (1 Thess. 5:17)? Are you praying in your prayer closet, hidden from the eyes of others? Are you praying always and everywhere? These are personal, pertinent, and all-important questions for every soul.

God's Word shows us, through many examples, that God intervenes in this world in answer to prayer. How clear it is, when the Bible is consulted, that the almighty God is brought directly into the things of this world by the prayers of His people. Jonah fled from duty and took ship for a distant port, but God followed him. By a strange providence this disobedient prophet was cast out of the ship, and the God who sent him to Nineveh prepared a fish to swallow him. In the fish's belly he cried out to the God against whom he had sinned, and God intervened and caused the fish to vomit Jonah out onto dry land. Even the fishes of the great deep are subject to the law of prayer.

The Weapon of Prayer by E. M. BOUNDS

DAY 2
ASK AND HAVE

*Ye lust, and have not: ye kill, and desire to have,
and cannot obtain: ye fight and war, yet ye have not,
because ye ask not. Ye ask, and receive not, because
ye ask amiss, that ye may consume it upon your lusts.*

JAMES 4:2,3

MAN IS a creature abounding in wants. He is ever restless. His heart is full of desires. I can hardly imagine a person who does not have many desires of some kind or another. Man is like a sea anemone with its multitude of tentacles, which are always hunting in the water for food. Man is like certain plants that send out tendrils, seeking to climb higher. Man steers for what he thinks to be his port, but, as yet, he is tossed about upon the waves. One of these days he hopes to find his heart's delight, and so he continues to desire with more or less expectancy.

This fact applies to both the worst of people and the best of people, but there is a difference between the desires of sinners and the desires of saints. Sinners' desires become lusts; their longings are selfish, sensual, and consequently evil. The current of their desires runs forcefully in a wrong direction. These lusts, in many cases, become extremely intense. They make the man their slave and domineer over his judgment; they stir him up to violence. He fights and wars, perhaps he literally kills.

At the same time, there are desires in Christians also. To rob the saints of their desires would be to injure them greatly, for by their desires they rise out of their lower selves. Believers desire the best things: things that are pure and peaceful, admirable and elevating. They desire God's glory; therefore, their motives are higher than the motives that inflame the unrenewed mind. Such desires in Christians are frequently very fervent and forceful. Indeed, they should always be so. Desires from the Spirit of God stir the renewed nature, exciting and stimulating it. They make the believer groan in anguish until he can attain the things that God has taught him to long for.

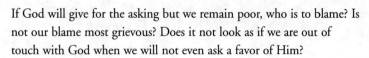

If God will give for the asking but we remain poor, who is to blame? Is not our blame most grievous? Does it not look as if we are out of touch with God when we will not even ask a favor of Him?

My fellow believers, whether we like it or not, asking is the rule of the kingdom. *"Ask, and ye shall receive"* (John 16:24). It is a rule that never will be altered in anybody's case.

Praying Successfully by CHARLES SPURGEON

DAY 3
WORSHIP

*And [he] pitched his tent, having Bethel on the west
and Hai on the east: and there he builded an altar.*

WORSHIP IS giving God the best that He has given you. Be careful what you do with the best you have. Whenever you get a blessing from God, give it back to Him as a love gift. Take time to meditate before God and offer the blessing back to Him in a deliberate act of worship. If you hoard a thing for yourself, it will turn into spiritual dry rot, as the manna did when it was hoarded. God will never let you hold a spiritual thing for yourself, it has to be given back to Him that He may make it a blessing to others.

Bethel is the symbol of communion with God; Hai is the symbol of the world. Abraham pitched his tent between the two. The measure of the worth of our public activity for God is the private profound communion we have with Him. Rush is wrong every time, there is always plenty of time to worship God. Quiet days with God may be a snare. We have to pitch our tents where we shall always have quiet times with God, however noisy our times with the world may be. There are not three stages in spiritual life—worship, waiting and work. Some of us go in jumps like spiritual frogs, we jump from worship to waiting, and from waiting to work. God's idea is that the three should go together. They were always together in the life of our Lord. He was unhasting and unresting. It is a discipline, we cannot get into it all at once.

My Utmost for His Highest by OSWALD CHAMBERS

EARNESTNESS
AND FAITH

I have not found so great faith, no, not in Israel.

LUKE 7:9

IF OUR prayer comes right from the heart, God understands our language. It is a delusion of the devil to think we cannot pray; we can, if we really want something. It is not the most beautiful or the most eloquent language that brings down the answer; it is the cry that goes up from a burdened heart. When this poor Gentile woman cried out, "Lord, help me!" the cry flashed over the divine wires, and the blessing came. You can pray if you will; it is the desire of the heart that God delights to hear and to answer.

In addition to being earnest, we must be expectant—we must expect to receive a blessing. When the centurion wanted Christ to heal his servant, he thought he was not worthy to go and ask the Lord himself, so he sent his friends to make the petition. He sent out messengers to meet the Master and say, "Don't trouble Yourself to come; all You have to do is to speak the word, and the disease will go." (See Luke 7:6-7) Jesus said to the Jews, *"I have not found so great faith, no, not in Israel"* (Luke 7:9). He marveled at the faith of this centurion; it pleased Him so much that He healed the servant right then. Faith brought the answer.

In John's gospel, we read of a nobleman whose child was sick. The father fell on his knees before the Master and said, *"Come down ere my child die"* (John 4:49). Here you have both earnestness and faith, and the Lord answered the prayer at once. The man's son began to recover that every hour. Christ honored the man's faith.

In his case, there was nothing to rest upon but the bare word of Christ, but this was enough. It is good to always bear in mind that the object of faith is not the creature, but the Creator; not the instrument, but the Hand that wields it.

The Joy of Answered Prayer by D. L. MOODY

DAY 5
THE TRUE WORSHIPPERS

The hour cometh, and now is, when the true worshippers
shall worship the Father in spirit and in truth: for the Father
seeketh such to worship him. God is a Spirit: and they that
worship him must worship him in spirit and in truth.

JOHN 4:23,24

THESE WORDS of Jesus to the woman of Samaria are His first
recorded teaching on the subject of prayer. They give us some wonderful first glimpses into the world of prayer. The Father *seeks* worshippers. Our worship satisfies His loving heart and is a joy to Him. He
seeks *true worshippers* but finds many who are not the way He would
like them. True worship is that which is *in spirit and truth*. The Son
has come to open the way for this worship in spirit and in truth, and
to teach it to us. One of our first lessons in the school of prayer must
be to understand what it is to pray in spirit and in truth and to know
how we can attain it.

To the woman of Samaria our Lord spoke of a three fold worship. First
there is the ignorant worship of the Samaritans: "Ye worship that which
ye know not." Second is the intelligent worship of the Jew, having the
true knowledge of God: "We worship that which we know; for salvation is of the Jews." The new, spiritual worship which He Himself has
come to introduce is third: "The hour is coming, and is now, when the
true worshippers shall worship the Father in spirit and truth."

The secret of prayer in spirit and truth is in the knowledge of the
Fatherhood of God, the revelation of His infinite Fatherliness in our
hearts, and the faith in His infinite love of us as His children. This is
the new and living way Christ opened up for us. To have Christ the
Son, and *the Spirit of the Son,* dwelling within us and revealing the
Father makes us true, spiritual worshippers.

With Christ in the School of Prayer by ANDREW MURRAY

THE LACK OF PRAYER

And He saw that there was no man, and
wondered that there was no intercessor.

ISAIAH 59:16

THE ENTIRE morning session of a convention I recently attended was devoted to prayer and intercession. Great blessing was found, both in listening to what the Word teaches of their need and power, and in joining in continued, united supplication. Many felt that we knew too little of persevering, importunate prayer, and that it is, indeed, one of the greatest needs of the Church.

We pray too little! There is even a lack of hope for any great change, due to force of habit, and the pressured feeling that prayer is a duty.

Imagine the difference between a man whose profits are just enough to maintain his family and keep up his business, and another whose income enables him to extend the business and to help others. There can be an earnest Christian life in which there is prayer enough to keep us from backsliding, just maintaining the position we have, without much growth in spirituality or Christlikeness. This prayer attitude is more defensive—seeking to ward off temptation—than aggressive, reaching out after higher attainment. If we are to grow in strength, with some large experience of God's power to sanctify ourselves and to bring down real blessing on others, there must be more definite and persevering prayer. The Scripture, teaching about "crying day and night;" "continuing steadfastly in prayer"; "watching unto prayer;" "being heard for his importunity," must, in some degree, become our experience if we are really to be intercessors.

Let us stir up the slumbering gift that is lying unused, and seek to gather, train, and band together as many as we can to be God's remembrancers, and to give Him no rest until He makes His Church a joy in the earth. Nothing but intense, believing prayer can meet the intense spirit of worldliness, which is complained of everywhere.

The Ministry of Intercession by ANDREW MURRAY

THE GLORIOUS PURSUIT

My soul followeth hard after thee: thy right hand upholdeth me.

PSALM 63:8

GOD IS a person, and in the deep of His mighty nature He thinks, wills, enjoys, feels, loves, desires and suffers as any other person may. In making Himself known to us He stays by the familiar pattern of personality. He communicates with us through the avenues of our minds, our wills and our emotions. The continuous and unembarrassed interchange of love and thought between God and the soul of the redeemed man is the throbbing heart of New Testament religion.

Come near to the holy men and women of the past and you will soon feel the heat of their desire after God. They mourned for Him; they prayed and wrestled and sought for Him day and night, in season and out, and when they had found Him the finding was all the sweeter for the long seeking. Moses used the fact that he knew God as an argument for knowing Him better. "Now therefore, I pray thee, if I have found grace in thy sight, show me now thy way, that I may know thee, that I may find grace in thy sight" (Exodus 33:13); and from there he rose to make the daring request, "I beseech thee, show me thy glory" (33:18). God was frankly pleased by this display of ardor, and the next day called Moses into the mount, and there in solemn procession made all His glory pass before him.

David's life was a torrent of spiritual desire, and his psalms ring with the cry of the seeker and the glad shout of the finder. Paul confessed the mainspring of his life to be his burning desire after Christ. "That I may know him" (Philippians 3:10) was the goal of his heart, and to this he sacrificed everything. "Yea doubtless, and I count all things but loss for the excellency of the knowledge of Christ Jesus my Lord: for whom I have suffered the loss of all things, and do count them but dung, that I may win Christ" (3:8).

Complacency is a deadly foe of all spiritual growth. Acute desire must be present or there will be no manifestation of Christ to His people.

The Pursuit of God, by A. W. TOZER

Compiled by EDYTHE DRAPER

ALL SPIRITUAL BLESSING

Blessed be the God and Father of our Lord Jesus Christ, who hath blessed us with all spiritual blessings in heavenly places in Christ.

EPHESIANS 1:3

JESUS CHRIST, by His atoning death and by His resurrection and ascension to the right hand of the Father, has obtained for every believer in Him every possible spiritual blessing. There is no spiritual blessing that any believer enjoys that may not be yours. It belongs to you now; Christ purchased it by His atoning death, and God has provided it in Him. It is there for you; but it is your part to claim it, to put out your hand and take it. God's appointed way of claiming blessings, or putting out your hand and taking hold of the blessings that are procured for you by the atoning death of Jesus Christ, is by prayer. Prayer is the hand that takes to ourselves the blessings that God has already provided in His Son.

Go through your Bible, and you will find it definitely stated that every conceivable spiritual blessing is obtained by prayer. For example, it is in answer to prayer, as we learn from Psalm 139:23-24, that God searches us and knows our hearts, tries us and knows our thoughts, brings to light the sin that there is in us and delivers us from it. As we learn from Psalm 19:12-13, it is in answer to prayer that we are cleansed from secret faults and God keeps us back from "presumptuous sins" (v. 13). It is in answer to prayer, as we learn from verse fourteen, that the words of our mouths and the meditations of our hearts are made acceptable in God's sight. And it is in answer to prayer, as we learn from Psalm 25:4-5, that God shows us His ways, teaches us His path, and guides us in His truth. We also learn from the prayer our Lord Himself taught us, that we are kept from temptation and delivered from the power of the "evil one" in answer to prayer (Matt. 6:14 RV). As we learn from Luke 11:13, it is in answer to prayer that God gives us His Holy Spirit. In this way, we might go on through the whole catalog of spiritual blessings, and we would find that every one is obtained by asking for it. Indeed, our Lord Himself has said in Matthew 7:11, "If ye then, being evil, know how to give good gifts unto your children, how much more shall your Father which is in heaven give good things to them that ask him?"

The Power of Prayer by R. A. TORREY

GRACE GUARANTEED

And it shall come to pass, that whosoever shall
call on the name of the LORD shall be delivered.

JOEL 2:32

If we want to understand the full meaning of Joel 2:32, let us first examine the circumstances at the time when Joel was writing. Vengeance was coming toward Judah at full speed. The armies of divine justice had been called forth for war. They ran like mighty men; they climbed the wall like men of war (Joel 2:7). They invaded and devastated the land, and they turned the land from being like the Garden of Eden into a desolate wilderness. All faces grew pale; the people were "much pained" (v. 6). The sun itself was dim, the moon was dark, and the stars withdrew themselves; furthermore, the earth quaked, and the heavens trembled (v. 10).

At such a dreadful time, when we might have least expected it, between the peals of thunder and the flashes of lightning was heard this gentle word: "It shall come to pass, that whosoever shall call on the name of the LORD shall be delivered."

In the worst times that can ever happen, salvation is still available. When day turns to night and life becomes death, when famine rules the land and the hope of man has fled, there still remains in God, in the person of His dear Son, deliverance to all who will call upon the name of the Lord.

We do not know what is going to happen. Looking into the future, I prophesy dark things. Even so, this light will always shine between the clouds: "Whosoever shall call on the name of the LORD shall be delivered."

I have nothing to write about except the old, old story of infinite mercy meeting infinite sin; of free grace leading free will into better things; of God Himself appearing to undo man's ruin that he brought on himself; of God lifting man up by a great deliverance.

—CHARLES SPURGEON

DAY 10
THE NECESSITY FOR PRAYING PEOPLE

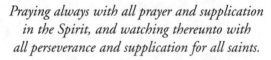

*Praying always with all prayer and supplication
in the Spirit, and watching thereunto with
all perseverance and supplication for all saints.*

EPHESIANS 6:18

ONE OF the most pressing needs in our day is for people whose faith, prayers, and study of the Word of God have been vitalized. We need people whose hearts have written on them a transcript of the Word. We need people who will give forth the Word as the incorruptible seed that lives and abides forever (1 Peter 1:23).

The church today needs praying people to meet the fearful crisis that is facing her. The crying need of the times is for people in increased numbers—God-fearing people, praying people, Holy Spirit people, people who can endure hardship. We need people who will not count their lives dear unto themselves (Acts 20:24) but count all things as loss for the excellency of the knowledge of Jesus Christ, the Savior (Phil. 3:8). The people who are so greatly needed in this age of the church are those who have learned the business of praying—learned it on their knees, learned it in the need and agony of their own hearts.

Praying people are the one commanding need of this day, as of all other days, if God is to intervene in the world.

In doing God's work there is no substitute for praying. People of prayer cannot be replaced with other kinds of people. People of financial skill, people of education, people of worldly influence—none of these can possibly substitute for people of prayer.

The people to whom Jesus Christ committed the fortunes and destiny of His church were people of prayer. To no other kind of people has God ever committed Himself.

—E. M. BOUNDS

DAY 11
WHAT'S THE GOOD OF PRAYER?

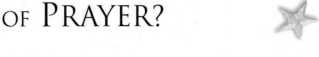

Lord, teach us to pray.

LUKE 11:1

IT IS not part of the life of a natural man to pray. We hear it said that a man will suffer in his life if he does not pray; I question it. What will suffer is the life of the Son of God in him, which is nourished not by food, but by prayer. When a man is born from above, the life of the Son of God is born in him, and he can either starve that life or nourish it. Prayer is the way the life of God is nourished. Our ordinary views of prayer are not found in the New Testament. We look upon prayer as a means of getting things for ourselves; the Bible idea of prayer is that we may get to know God Himself.

"Ask and ye shall receive." We grouse before God, we are apologetic or apathetic, but we ask very few things. Yet what a splendid audacity a childlike child has! Our Lord says—"Except ye become as little children." Ask, and God will do. Give Jesus Christ a chance, give Him elbow room, and no man will ever do this unless he is at his wits' end. When a man is at his wits' end it is not a cowardly thing to pray, it is the only way he can get into touch with Reality. Be yourself before God and present your problems, the things you know you have come to your wits' end over. As long as you are self-sufficient, you do not need to ask God for anything.

It is not so true that "prayer changes things" as that prayer changes *me* and I change things. God has so constituted things that prayer on the basis of Redemption alters the way in which a man looks at things. Prayer is not a question of altering things externally, but of working wonders in a man's disposition.

—OSWALD CHAMBERS

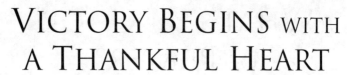

DAY 12
VICTORY BEGINS WITH A THANKFUL HEART

In every thing give thanks: for this is the
will of God in Christ Jesus concerning you.

I THESSALONIANS 5:18

WE OUGHT to be more thankful for what we receive from God. Perhaps some of you who are mothers have a child in your family who is constantly complaining, never thankful. You know that there is not much pleasure in doing anything for a child like that. If you meet a beggar who is always grumbling and never seem to be thankful for what you give, you very soon shut the door in his face altogether. Ingratitude is about the hardest thing we have to deal with. Shakespeare wrote,

> Blow, blow, thou winter wind,
> Thou art not so unkind
> As man's ingratitude;
> Thy tooth is not so keen,
> Because thou art not seen,
> Although thy breath be rude.

We cannot speak too plainly of this evil, which so demeans those who are guilty of it. Even in Christians there is too much ingratitude! Here we are, getting blessings from God day after day, yet how little praise and thanksgiving there is in the church of God!

It is said that in a time of great despondency among the first settlers in New England, it was proposed in one of their public assemblies to proclaim a fast. An old farmer arose. He spoke of their provoking heaven with their complaints. He reviewed their measures, showed that they had much to be thankful for, and moved that instead of appointing a day of fasting, they should appoint a day of thanksgiving. This was done, and the custom has been continued ever since.

Among all the apostles, none suffered as much as Paul, but none of them do we find giving thanks as often as he. Take his letter to the Philippians for an example. Remember what he suffered at Philippi, how they beat him with many blows and cast him into prison. Yet every chapter in this epistle speaks of rejoicing and giving thanks.

Even if we had nothing else to be thankful for, we would always have ample cause for giving thanks in that Jesus Christ loved us and gave Himself for us (Gal. 2:20).

—D. L. MOODY

DAY 13
THE WORD AND PRAYER

*If ye abide in me, and my words abide in you, ye shall
ask what ye will, and it shall be done unto you.*

JOHN 15:7

THE VITAL connection between the Word and prayer is one of the
simplest and earliest lessons of the Christian life. As that newly-con-
verted heathen put it: "I pray—I speak to my Father; I read—my
Father speaks to me." Before prayer, God's Word strengthens me by
giving my faith its justification and its petition. And after prayer,
God's Word prepares me by revealing what the Father wants me to
ask. In prayer, God's Word brings me the answer, for in it the Spirit
allows me to hear the Father's voice.

Prayer is not monologue, but dialogue. Its most essential part is God's
voice in response to mine. Listening to God's voice is the secret of the
assurance that He will listen to mine. "Incline thine ear and hear,"
"Give ear to me," and "Hearken to my voice," are words which God
speaks to man as well as man to God. His hearkening will depend on
ours. My willingness to accept His words will determine the power my
words have with Him. What God's words are to me is the test of what
He Himself is to me. It shows the uprightness of my desire to meet
Him in prayer.

When God reveals Himself in His words, He does indeed give
Himself—His love and His life, His will and His power—to those who
receive these words, in a reality passing comprehension. In every
promise, He gives us the power to grasp and possess *Himself.* In every
command, He allows us to share His will, His holiness, and His per-
fection. God's Word gives us God Himself.

—ANDREW MURRAY

DAY 14
THE POWER OF GRACE

Wretched man that I am! Who shall deliver me from the body
of this death? I thank God through Jesus Christ our Lord....
The law of the Spirit of life in Christ Jesus hath
made me free from the law of sin and death.

ROMANS 7:24,25; 8:2

A GENTLEMAN once came to me for advice and help. He was evidently an earnest and well-instructed Christian man. For several years, he had been in quite difficult surroundings, trying to witness for Christ. The result was a sense of failure and unhappiness. His complaint was that he had no relish for the Word, and that, though he prayed, it was as if his heart was not in it. If he spoke to others, or gave a tract, it was under a sense of duty; the love and the joy were not present. He longed to be filled with God's Spirit, but the more he sought it, the farther off it appeared to be. What was he to think of his state, and was there any way out of it?

My answer was that the whole matter appeared to be very simple: he was living under the law and not under grace. As long as he did so, there could be no change. He listened attentively, but could not see exactly what I meant.

I reminded him of the difference, the absolute contrast between law and grace. Law demands; grace bestows. Law commands, but gives no strength to obey. Grace promises and performs, doing everything for us. Law burdens, casts down, and condemns. Grace comforts, makes strong and glad. Law appeals to self to do its utmost; grace points to Christ to do all. Law requires effort and strain, urging us toward a goal we can never reach. Grace works all of God's blessed will in us. I pointed out to him how his first step should be to completely accept his failure and his inability, as God had been trying to show him, instead of striving against it. With this acceptance and confession, he could sink down before God in utter helplessness. There he would learn that, unless grace gave him deliverance and strength, he could never do better than he had done, and that grace would, indeed, work all for him. He must come out from under law, self, and effort, taking his place under grace and allowing God to do all.

—ANDREW MURRAY

DAY 15
CULTIVATING
SPIRITUAL RECEPTIVITY

Seek ye the LORD while he may be found,
call ye upon him while he is near.

ISAIAH 55:6

WHY DO some persons "find" God in a way that others do not? Why does God manifest His presence to some and let multitudes of others struggle along in the half-light of imperfect Christian experience? Of course, the will of God is the same for all. He has no favorites within His household. All He has ever done for any of His children He will do for all of His children. The difference lies not with God but with us.

Pick at random a score of great saints whose lives and testimonies are widely known. Let them be Bible characters or well-known Christians of post-biblical times. You will be struck instantly with the fact that the saints were not alike. Sometimes the dissimilarities were so great as to be positively glaring. How different, for example, was Moses from Isaiah; how different was Elijah from David; how unlike each other were John and Paul, St. Francis and Luther, Finney and Thomas à Kempis. The differences are as wide as human life itself—differences of race, nationality, education, temperament, habit and personal qualities. Yet they all walked, each in his day, upon a high road of spiritual living far above the common way.

Their differences must have been incidental and in the eyes of God of no significance. In some vital quality they must have been alike. What was it?

I venture to suggest that the one vital quality which they had in common was *spiritual receptivity.* Something in them was open to heaven, something which urged them Godward. I shall say simply that they had spiritual awareness and that they went on to cultivate it until it became the biggest thing in their lives. They differed from the average person in that when they felt the inward longing they *did something about it.* They acquired the lifelong habit of spiritual response.

—A. W. TOZER

DAY 16
PRAYING in the NAME of JESUS

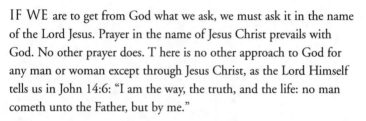

Whatsoever ye shall ask in my name, that will I do,
that the Father may be glorified in the Son.
If ye shall ask any thing in my name, I will do it.

JOHN 14:13,14

IF WE are to get from God what we ask, we must ask it in the name of the Lord Jesus. Prayer in the name of Jesus Christ prevails with God. No other prayer does. T here is no other approach to God for any man or woman except through Jesus Christ, as the Lord Himself tells us in John 14:6: "I am the way, the truth, and the life: no man cometh unto the Father, but by me."

But just what does it mean to pray in the name of Jesus?

Suppose I were to walk into a bank at which I do not have an account. I write out a check, "Pay to the order of R. A. Torrey the sum of five dollars." Then I sign my own name at the bottom of the check, go to the teller's window, and ask to cash that check. What would I be doing? I would be asking that bank to give me five dollars. And in whose name would I be asking it? In my own name. And what would happen? T he teller would take the check and look at it, and then look at me, and then he would say, "Dr. Torrey, do you have an account at this bank?"

"No."

Then what would the teller say? Something like this: "We would like to accommodate you, but that is not good business. You have no claim whatsoever on this bank, and we cannot honor your check even though it is for only five dollars."

Now that is exactly what praying in the name of Jesus Christ means. It means that we go to the Bank of Heaven, on which neither you nor I nor any other man on earth has any claim of his own, but upon which

137

Jesus Christ has infinite claims. In Jesus' name, which He has given us a right to put on our checks, if we are united to Him by a living faith that reveals itself in an obedient love, we may ask whatever we need. Or, to put it another way, to pray in the name of Jesus Christ is to recognize that we have no claims on God whatsoever, that God owes us nothing whatsoever, that we deserve nothing from God; but, believing what God Himself tells us about Jesus Christ's claims upon Him, we ask God for things on the ground of Jesus Christ's claims upon God. And when we draw near to God in that way, we can get "whatsoever we ask," no matter how great it may be.

—R. A. TORREY

DAY 17
PRAY FOR OTHERS

*Moreover as for me, God forbid that I should sin
against the LORD in ceasing to pray for you.*

I SAMUEL 12:23

CHRISTIAN PEOPLE must pray for others. On one occasion
Samuel said to the people, "Moreover as for me, God forbid that I
should sin against the LORD in ceasing to pray for you" (1 Sam.
12:23). Fortunately, these sinful Israelites, who had rejected God and
desired a human king, had a man of prayer.

One way to increase personal grace is to pray for others. Intercessory
prayer is a means of grace to those who exercise it. It is in the paths of
intercessory prayer that we enter the richest fields of spiritual growth
and gather priceless riches. To pray for others is of divine appoint-
ment, and it represents the highest form of Christian service.

People must pray, and people must be prayed for. The Christian must
pray for all things, of course, but prayers for people are infinitely more
important, just as people are infinitely more important than things.
Also, prayers for people are far more important than prayers for things
because people more deeply involve God's will and the work of Jesus
Christ. People are to be cared for, sympathized with, and prayed for,
because sympathy, pity, compassion, and care accompany and precede
prayer for people.

All this makes praying a real business, not child's play, not a secondary
affair, not a trivial matter, but a serious business. The people who have
made a success of praying have made a business of praying. It is a process
demanding the time, thought, energy, and hearts of mankind. Prayer is
business for time, business for eternity. It is our business to pray, tran-
scending all other business and taking precedence over all other vocations,
professions, or occupations. Our praying concerns not only ourselves, but
all people and their greatest interests, and even the salvation of their
immortal souls. Praying is a business that takes hold of eternity and the
things beyond the grave. It is a business that involves earth and heaven. All
worlds are touched by prayer, and all worlds are influenced by prayer.

—E. M. BOUNDS

DAY 18
HOW TO TAKE ADVANTAGE OF ADVERSITY

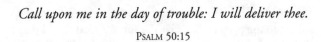

Call upon me in the day of trouble: I will deliver thee.

PSALM 50:15

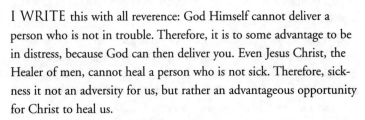

I WRITE this with all reverence: God Himself cannot deliver a person who is not in trouble. Therefore, it is to some advantage to be in distress, because God can then deliver you. Even Jesus Christ, the Healer of men, cannot heal a person who is not sick. Therefore, sickness it not an adversity for us, but rather an advantageous opportunity for Christ to heal us.

The point is, my reader, your adversity may prove your advantage by offering occasion for the display of divine grace. It is wise to learn the art of making lemonade out of lemons, and the text teaches us how to do that. It shows how trouble can become gain. When you are in adversity, t hen call upon God, and you will experience a deliverance that will be a richer and sweeter experience for your soul than if you had never known trouble. It is an art and a science to make gains out of losses, and advantages out of adversities.

—CHARLES SPURGEON

DAY 19

THE UNRIVALED
POWER OF PRAYER

We know not what we should pray for as we ought:
but the Spirit itself maketh intercession for us
with groanings which cannot be uttered.

ROMANS 8:26

WE REALIZE that we are energized by the Holy Spirit for prayer;
we know what it is to pray in the Spirit; but we do not so often realize
that the Holy Spirit Himself prays in us prayers which we cannot
utter. When we are born again of God and are indwelt by the Spirit of
God, He expresses for us the unutterable.

"He [the Spirit in you] maketh intercession for the saints according to the
will of God," and God searches your heart not to know what your conscious prayers are, but to find out what is the prayer of the Holy Spirit.

The Spirit of God needs the nature of the believer as a shrine in which
to offer His intercession. "Your body is the temple of the Holy Ghost."
When Jesus Christ cleansed the temple, He "would not suffer that any
man should carry any vessel through the temple." The Spirit of God
will not allow you to use your body for your own convenience. Jesus
ruthlessly cast out all them that sold and bought in the temple, and
said, "My house shall be called the house of prayer; but ye have made
it a den of thieves."

Have we recognized that our body is the temple of the Holy Ghost? If
so, we must be careful to keep it undefiled for Him. We have to
remember that our conscious life, though it is only a tiny bit of our
personality, is to be regarded by us as a shrine of the Holy Ghost. He
will look after the unconscious part that we know nothing of; but we
must see that we guard the conscious part for which we are responsible.

—OSWALD CHAMBERS

DAY 20
THE POWER OF CONFESSION

*Search me, O God, and know my heart: try me,
and know my thoughts: and see if there be any
wicked way in me, and lead me in the way everlasting.*

PSALM 139:23,24

YOUR PRAYERS are answered when your heart is right with God.

The men who lived nearest to God and had the most power with Him
were those who confessed their sins and failures. Daniel, as we have
seen, confessed his sins and those of his people (see Daniel 9:20). Yet
there is nothing recorded against Daniel. He was one of the best men
on the face of the earth, yet his confession of sin was one of the
deepest and most humble on record.

Job was no doubt a holy man, a mighty prince, yet he had to fall in
the dust and confess his sins. You will find the necessity of confession
all through the Bible. When Isaiah saw the purity and holiness of
God, he beheld himself in his true state and exclaimed, "Woe is me!
For I am undone; because I am a man of unclean lips" (Isaiah 6:5).

I firmly believe that the Church of God will have to confess her own
sins before there can be any great work of grace. There must be a deeper
work among God's believing people. I sometimes think it is about time
to give up preaching to the ungodly and preach to those who profess to
be Christians. If we had a higher standard of life in the church of God,
there would be thousands more flocking into the kingdom.

The prayer of the humble, contrite heart is a delight to God. There is
no sound that goes up from this sin-cursed earth that is so sweet to
His ear as the prayer of the man who is walking uprightly.

—D. L. MOODY

DAY 21
THE POWER OF
UNITED PRAYER

Again I say unto you, That if two of you shall agree on earth as touching any thing that they shall ask, it shall be done for them of my Father which is in heaven. For where two or three are gathered together in my name, there am I in the midst of them.

MATTHEW 18:19,20

GOD GIVES us a very special promise for the united prayer of two or three who agree in what they ask. As a tree has its root hidden in the ground and its stem growing up into the sunlight, so prayer needs secrecy in which the soul meets God alone *and* public fellowship with those who find their common meeting place in the Name of Jesus.

The reason why this must be so is plain. The bond that unites a man with his fellow-men is no less real and close that that which unites him to God: He is one with them. Grace renews not only our relationship with God, but our relationships with our fellow human beings, too. We not only learn to say "My Father." It would be unnatural for the children of a family to always meet their father separately, never expressing their desires or their love jointly. Believers are not only members of one family, but of one body. Just as each member of the Body depends on the other, the extent to which the Spirit can dwell in the Body depends on the union and cooperation of everyone. Christians cannot reach the full blessing God is ready to bestow through His Spirit until they seek and receive it in fellowship with each other. It was to the hundred and twenty praying together in total agreement under the same roof that the Spirit came from the throne of the glorified Lord. In the same way, it is in the union and fellowship of believers that the Spirit can manifest His full power.

—ANDREW MURRAY

DAY 22
MY GOD WILL HEAR ME

I have called upon Thee, for Thou wilt hear me, O God.

PSALM 17:6

THE POWER of prayer rests in the faith that God hears it. In more than one sense, this is true. It is this faith that gives a man courage to pray. It is this faith that gives him power to prevail with God. The moment I am assured that God hears *me,* too, I feel drawn to pray and to persevere in prayer. I feel the strength to claim and take in faith the answer God gives. The main reason for the lack of prayer is the want of the living, joyous assurance: "My God will hear me." If only God's servants had a vision of the living God waiting to grant their request—to bestow all the heavenly gifts of the Spirit they are in need of—how everything would be set aside to make room for this one power that can ensure heavenly blessing—the pray of faith!

When a man can and does say, in living faith, "My God will hear me!" nothing can keep him from prayer. He knows that what he cannot do or get done on earth, can and will be done for him from heaven. Let each one of us bow in stillness before God, and wait on Him to reveal Himself to us as the prayer-bearing God. Ion His presence, the wondrous thoughts gathering round the central truth will be revealed to us.

—*The Ministry of Intercession* by ANDREW MURRAY

DAY 23
ENTERING THE
HOLY OF HOLIES

*I will hear what God the LORD will speak: for he will speak
peace unto his people, and to his saints.*

PSALM 85:8

THE INTERIOR journey of the soul from the wilds of sin into the
enjoyed presence of God is beautifully illustrated in the Old Testament
tabernacle. The returning sinner first entered the outer court where he
offered a blood sacrifice on the brazen altar and washed himself in the
laver that stood near it. Then he passed through a veil into the holy
place where no natural light could come, but the golden candlestick
which spoke of Jesus, the Light of the World, threw its soft glow over
all. There also was the shewbread to tell of Jesus, the Bread of Life,
and the altar of incense, a figure of unceasing prayer.

Though the worshiper had enjoyed so much, still he had not yet
entered the presence of God. Another veil separated from the Holy of
Holies where above the mercy seat dwelt the very God Himself in
awful and glorious manifestation. While the tabernacle stood, only the
high priest could enter there, and that but once a year, with blood
which he offered for his sins and the sins of the people. It was this last
veil which was rent when our Lord gave up the ghost on Calvary, and
the sacred writer explains that this rending of the veil opened the way
for every worshiper in the world to come by the new and living way
straight into the divine Presence.

Everything in the New Testament accords with this Old Testament
picture. Ransomed men need no longer pause in fear to enter the Holy
of Holies. *God wills that we should push on into His presence and live
our whole life there.* This is to be known to us in conscious experience.
It is more than a doctrine to be held; it is a life to be enjoyed every
moment of every day.

—A. W. TOZER

DAY 24
SIN IN THE HEART OR LIFE

Behold, the LORD's hand is not shortened, that it cannot save;
neither his ear heavy, that it cannot hear: but your iniquities
have separated between you and your God, and your sins have
hid his face from you, that he will not hear.

ISAIAH 59:1,2

WE ARE distinctly told that in many instances, the reason why God does not answer prayer is that our iniquities and our sins have separated us from our God, and hidden His face from us, so that He will not hear. The people of Isaiah's time were saying, "God does not answer prayer any longer. He may have answered it in the days of Moses; He may have answered in the days of Elijah, but He does not answer any longer. Either His ear is heavy that it cannot hear, or His hand is shortened that it cannot save."

"No, no," said Isaiah, "the LORD's hand is not shortened, that it cannot save: neither his ear heavy, that it cannot hear" (Isa. 59:1). The trouble is not with God; the trouble is with you. "Your iniquities have separated between you and your God, and your sins have hid his face from you, that he will not hear" (v. 2). Sin in our hearts or lives makes it impossible for God to answer our prayer, even though the thing for which we are praying is entirely according to His will.

If you are praying for something and you do not get it, do not conclude that God does not answer prayer; do not conclude that God does not answer prayer today as He did in the olden times; do not conclude that this thing that you are asking for is not according to the will of God. Get alone with God, ask Him to search your heart, and ask Him to show you whether there is anything in your past life that you have done that was wrong that you have not set straight, any past sin that you have not judged, or whether there is anything in your life today that is displeasing to Him. And then wait silently before Him and give Him an opportunity to show you. If He shows you anything, confess it to Him as sin and give it up.

When He shows you, set it straight at once, and you will find an open heaven and a God who answers prayer—a God whose ear is not only quick to hear prayer in general, and whose hand is not only strong to save in general, but a God whose ear is quick to hear your prayer, and whose hand is long and strong to give immediate deliverance to you. Oh, how many things there are that we greatly need and that we might have at once if we would only judge and put away our sin!

—R. A. TORREY

DAY 25
PRAYER PUTS GOD TO WORK

From of old no one has heard or perceived by the ear, no eye has seen a God besides thee, who works for those who wait for him.

ISAIAH 64:4 (RSV)

PRAYER AFFECTS three different spheres of existence: the divine, the angelic, and the human. It puts God to work, it puts angels to work, and it puts people to work. It lays its hands upon God, angels, and people. What a wonderful reach there is in prayer! It brings into play the forces of heaven and earth. God, angels, and people are subjects of this wonderful law of prayer, and all three deal with the possibilities and the results of prayer.

God has placed Himself under the law of prayer to such an extent that He is induced to work among people in a way in which He does not work if they do not pray. Prayer takes hold of God and influences Him to work. This is the meaning of prayer as it concerns God. This is the doctrine of prayer, or else there is no value whatsoever in prayer.

Prayer puts God to work in all things prayed for. While man in his weakness and poverty waits, trusts, and prays, God undertakes the work. "From of old no one has heard or perceived by the ear, no eye has seen a God besides thee, who works for those who wait for him" (Isa. 64 RSV).

Jesus Christ commits Himself to the force of prayer. "Whatsoever ye shall ask in my name," He says, "that will I do, that the Father may be glorified in the Son. If ye shall ask any thing in my name, I will do it" (John 14:13-14). And, again, "If ye abide in me, and my words abide in you, ye shall ask what ye will, and it shall be done unto you" (John 15:7).

The promise of God is committed to nothing as strongly as it is to prayer. The purposes of God are not dependent on any other force as much as this force of prayer.

—E. M. BOUNDS

DAY 26
DAVID'S PRAYER
IN THE CAVE

A prayer when he was in the cave.

PSALM 142:1

I LIKE the title given to Psalm 142: "A prayer when he was in the cave." David did pray when he was in the cave. If he had prayed half as much when he was in the palace as he did when he was in the cave, things would have been better for him. But, alas, when he was king, we find him rising from his bed in the evening, looking from the roof of his house, and falling into temptation. If he had been looking up to heaven, if his heart had been in communion with God, he might never have committed that great crime that has so deeply stained his whole character.

"A prayer when he was in the cave." God will hear prayer on the land, on the sea, and even under the sea. I remember someone at a prayer meeting saying so. Somebody else at the prayer meeting was rather astonished and asked, "How could God hear prayer under the sea?" The man said that he was a diver, and he often went down to the bottom of the sea after shipwrecks. He said that he had held communion with God while he had been at work in the depths of the ocean.

Our God is not only the God of the hills, but also of the valleys. He is the God of both land and sea. He heard Jonah when the disobedient prophet was at the roots of the mountains and when "the earth with her bars" (Jonah 2:6) seemed to be around him forever. Wherever you work, you can pray. Wherever you lie sick, you can pray. There is no place to which you can be banished that God is not near, and there is no time of day or night that His throne is inaccessible.

—CHARLES SPURGEON

DAY 27

THINK AS
JESUS TAUGHT

Pray without ceasing.

I Thessalonians 5:17

WE THINK rightly or wrongly about prayer according to the conception we have in our minds of prayer. If we think of prayer as the breath in our lungs and the blood from our hearts, we think rightly. The blood flows ceaselessly, and breathing continues ceaselessly; we are not conscious of it, but it is always going on. We are not always conscious of Jesus keeping us in perfect joint with God, but if we are obeying Him, He always is. Prayer is not an exercise, it is the life. Beware of anything that stops ejaculatory prayer. "Pray without ceasing," keep the childlike habit of ejaculatory prayer in your heart to God all the time.

Jesus never mentioned unanswered prayer; He had the boundless certainty that prayer is always answered. Have we by the Spirit the unspeakable certainty that Jesus had about prayer, or do we think of the times when God does not seem to have answered prayer? "Every one that asketh receiveth." We say, "But, but…" God answers prayer in the best way, not sometimes, but every time, although the immediate manifestation of the answer in the domain in which we want it may not always follow. Do we expect God to answer prayer?

The danger with us is that we want to water down the things that Jesus says and make them mean something in accordance with common sense; if it were only common sense, it was not worthwhile for Him to say it. The things Jesus says about prayer are supernatural revelations.

—OSWALD CHAMBERS

DAY 28
YOU CAN MAKE A DIFFERENCE

Father, I thank thee that thou hast heard me. And I knew that thou hearest me always: but because of the people which stand by I said it, that they may believe that thou hast sent me.

JOHN 11:41,42

THOSE WHO have left the deepest impression on this sin-cursed earth have been men and women of prayer. You will find that prayer has been the mighty power that has moved not only God, but man also.

Abraham was a man of prayer, and angels came down from heaven to converse with him.

Jacob's prayer was answered in the wonderful interview at Peniel, which resulted in his having such a mighty blessing, and in softening the heart of his brother Esau (see Genesis 32:24-30; 33:4).

The child Samuel was given in answer to Hannah's prayer (see 1 Samuel 1:9-11, 20).

Elijah's prayer closed up the heavens for three years and six months, and he prayed again and the heavens gave rain (See 1 Kings 17:1; 18:41-45, and James 5:17-18).

We read that, on another occasion, Elijah brought fire down on Mount Carmel (see 1 Kings 18:17-39). The prophets of Baal cried long and loud, but no answer came. The God of Elijah heard and answered his prayer. Let us remember that the God of Elijah still lives. As we go to the throne of grace, let us always remember that God answers prayer.

All through the Scriptures you will find that when believing prayer went up to God, the answer came down.

—D. L. MOODY

Prayer will Save Others

*If any man see his brother sin a sin which is not
unto death, he shall ask, and he shall give
him life for them that sin not unto death.*

1 John 5:16

THIS IS one of the most remarkable statements in the whole Bible on the subject of prayer and its amazing power. The statement of this verse is not only most remarkable, but it is also most cheering and most gladdening. Here God tells us that prayer will not only bring blessing to the one who prays, but that it will also bring the greatest of all blessings to others, even the blessing of eternal life to those for whom we pray. It tells us that if we see another sinning a sin not unto death— that is, committing sin, any sin except the one unpardonable sin—we can go to God in prayer for that person, and in answer to our prayers, God will give eternal life to this one for whom we have prayed.

We can accomplish more for the salvation of others by praying for them than we can in any other way. I do not mean by this that when we feel our responsibility for the salvation of someone else we should merely pray for them and do nothing else.

Prayer will reach down, down, down into the deepest depths of sin and ruin and take hold of men and women who seem lost beyond all possibility or hope of redemption, and lift them up, up, up until they are fit for a place beside the Son of God upon the throne.

—R. A. TORREY

DAY 30
PRAYER MUST BE SPECIFIC

And Jesus answered and said unto him,
What wilt thou that I should do unto thee?

MARK 10:51

THE BLIND man had been crying out loud repeatedly, "Thou Son of David, have mercy on me." The cry had reached the ear of the Lord. He knew what the man wanted and was ready to grant it to him. But before He did it, He asked him, *"What wilt thou* that I should do unto thee?" He wanted to hear not only the general petition for mercy, but the distinct expression of what the man's desire was that day. Until he verbalized it, he was not healed.

There are still petitioners to whom the Lord puts the same question who cannot get the aid they need until they answer that question. Our prayers must be a distinct expression of definite need, not a vague appeal to His mercy or an indefinite cry for blessing. It isn't that His loving heart does not understand or is not ready to hear our cry. Rather, Jesus desires such definite prayer for our own sakes because it teaches us to know our own needs better. Time, thought, and self-scrutiny are required to find out what our greatest need really is. Our desires are put to the test to see whether they are honest and real and are according to God's Word. We also consider whether we really believe we will receive the things we ask. Such reflective prayer helps us to wait for the special answer and to mark it when it comes.

So much of our prayer is vague and pointless. Some cry for mercy, but do not take the trouble to know exactly why they want it. Others ask to be delivered from sin, but do not name any sin from which a deliverance can be claimed. Still others pray for God's blessing on those around them—for the outpouring of God's Spirit on their land or on the world—and yet have no special field where they can wait and expect to see the answer. To everyone the Lord says, "What do you really want, and what do you expect Me to do?"

—ANDREW MURRAY

DAY 31
MY PRAYER

I urge you, first of all, to pray for all people. As you make your requests, plead for God's mercy upon them, and give thanks.

1 TIMOTHY 2:1

O MY Blessed High Priest! Who am I that You should invite me to share Your power of intercession? And why, O my Lord, am I so slow of heart to understand, believe, and exercise this wonderful privilege to which You have redeemed Your people? O Lord! Give me Your grace, that my life's work may become praying without ceasing, to draw down the blessing of heaven on all my surroundings on earth.

Blessed Lord! I come now to accept my calling, for which I will give up everything and follow You. Into Your hands I will believingly yield my whole being. Form, train, and inspire me to be one of Your prayer force, those who watch and strive in prayer, who have power and victory. Take possession of my heart, and fill it with the desire to glorify God in the gathering, sanctification, and union of those whom the Father has given You. Take my mind and give me wisdom to know when prayer can bring a blessing. Take me wholly and prepare me as You would a priest, to stand always before God and to bless His Name.

Blessed Lord! Now and through all my spiritual life, let me want everything for You, and nothing for myself. Let it be my experience that the person who has and asks for nothing for himself, receives everything, including the wonderful grace of sharing Your everlasting ministry of intercession. Amen.

—ANDREW MURRAY

PRAYER OF SALVATION

God loves you—no matter who you are, no matter what your past. God loves you so much that He gave His one and only begotten Son for you. The Bible tells us that "...whoever believes in him shall not perish but have eternal life" (John 3:16 NIV). Jesus laid down His life and rose again so that we could spend eternity with Him in heaven and experience His absolute best on earth. If you would like to receive Jesus into your life, say the following prayer out loud and mean it from your heart.

> *Heavenly Father, I come to You admitting that I am a sinner. Right now, I choose to turn away from sin, and I ask You to cleanse me of all unrighteousness. I believe that Your Son, Jesus, died on the cross to take away my sins. I also believe that He rose again from the dead so that I might be forgiven of my sins and made righteous through faith in Him. I call upon the name of Jesus Christ to be the Savior and Lord of my life. Jesus, I choose to follow You and ask that You fill me with the power of the Holy Spirit. I declare that right now I am a child of God. I am free from sin and full of the righteousness of God. I am saved in Jesus' name. Amen.*

If you prayed this prayer to receive Jesus Christ as your Savior for the first time, please contact us on the web at www.whitestonebooks.com to receive a free book.

Or you may write to us at:

White Stone Books

P.O. Box 35035

Tulsa, Oklahoma 74153

RESOURCES

The Joy of Answered Prayer by D. L. Moody

The Ministry of Intercession by Andrew Murray

My Utmost for His Highest by Oswald Chambers

The Power of Prayer by R. A. Torrey

Praying Successfully by Charles Spurgeon

The Pursuit of God by A. W. Tozer (compiled by Edythe Draper)

The Weapon of Prayer by E. M. Bounds

With Christ in the School of Prayer by Andrew Murray

OTHER TITLES BY
WHITE STONE BOOKS

Scriptural Prayers for the Praying Man

Scriptural Prayers for the Praying Teen

Scriptural Prayers for the Praying Woman

Scriptural Prayers for the Praying Mother

The Family Blessing, by Rolf Garborg

Additional copies of this book are
available from your local bookstore.

*"He who has an ear, let him hear what the Spirit says to
the churches. To him who overcomes, I will give some
of the hidden manna. I will also give him
a white stone with a new name written on it,
known only to him who receives it."*

WHITE STONE BOOKS
LAKELAND, FLORIDA